# CBEST Writing Study Guide
## Expanded Edition

# with Sample CBEST Essays,
# CBEST English Grammar Review Workbook, and
# Essay Correction Exercises for the
# California Basic Educational Skills Test

**CBEST Writing Study Guide Expanded Edition: with Sample CBEST Essays, CBEST English Grammar Review Workbook, and Essay Correction Exercises for the California Basic Educational Skills Test**

© COPYRIGHT 2015, 2021. Exam SAM Study Aids & Media dba www.examsam.com

ISBN: 978-1-949282-75-7

For information on bulk discounts, please contact Exam SAM via our webpage.

# TABLE OF CONTENTS

## PART 1 – About the CBEST Essays:

## PART 2 - Writing the CBEST Expository Essay:

# PART 1 – ABOUT THE CBEST ESSAYS

## CBEST Essay Format & Question Types

CBEST essay writing

Your CBEST test will include a written essay.

The purpose of the essay is to assess your ability to express and develop your thoughts in writing.

The essay assesses this skill because clear writing is essential for a successful teaching career.

Test administration

You may be asked to write your essay on paper or on a computer.

If you are asked to write your essay on a computer, you can ask for scratch paper to take notes and plan your essay.

Study aids, such as dictionaries or grammar books, are not permitted.

Time limit

Normally, you will be given 30 minutes to plan, write, and edit each of your two CBEST essays.

Word count

Although there is no official word limit, your essays should normally be between 300 to 450 words each.

# The CBEST Expository Essay Task

Your first CBEST essay question is an expository task.

For the expository task, you will have to analyze a statement, and then give reasons for the opinions you have expressed.

In other words, you will need to take a stand on the issue presented and support your viewpoint with reasons and examples.

The expository essay is designed to allow you to demonstrate your analytical skills.

Note that you will not be expected to demonstrate specialist knowledge in any particular academic subject area for your expository essay response.

Here is a sample expository essay question:

Most Americans have access to computers and cell phones on a daily basis, making email and text messaging extremely popular. While some people argue that email and texting are now the most convenient forms of personal communication, others believe that electronic communication technology is often used inappropriately. Write an essay for an audience of educated adults in which you take a position on this topic. Be sure to provide reasons and examples to support your viewpoint.

*We will see sample responses to this essay topic in the second part of the study guide.*

## The CBEST Personal Experience Essay Task

The second CBEST essay task is a personal experience piece.

You will be required to write about a personal experience you have faced.

The personal experience essay topic is designed to elicit expressive writing about an experience that you remember well.

In other words, the aim of this task is expressive writing, so you can make your tone much more personal than in essay 1.

For this reason, most students find essay task 2 much easier to write than essay task 1.

If permitted to do so, you may therefore wish to write task 2 before attempting task 1 on the day of your actual CBEST test.

Note that you will not be asked to write letters or other forms of correspondence for the CBEST personal experience essay.

You will also not be asked to write about a hypothetical or imaginary situation for this essay task.

*We will see sample personal experience essay topics and model responses in the third part of the study guide.*

# Essay Scoring – How Your CBEST Essays Are Marked

The six following characteristics of your CBEST essays will be assessed:

1. <u>Clear central idea</u> – This means that your essay should answer the question that has been posed. You will need to express your main idea in a clear way in the introduction of the essay. The scorer reading your essay assesses this aspect of your essay by searching for a thesis statement in the first paragraph of your essay.

2. <u>Well-supported</u> – Your essays should demonstrate unity and coherence among the examples that you use to support your argument.

   For the expository essay, you need to be sure that you take a stand on one side of the issue or the other. Your score will not be affected by the position you take.

   For the personal experience piece, it is extremely important to elaborate on the main idea of your essay and maintain your point of view throughout your writing.

   Your essays should include examples and explanations that illustrate and support your viewpoints.

The scorer reading your essays searches for linking words and phrases that signal that examples or reasons are being provided in the essay. These linking words and phrases include the following: "such as," "for example," "for this reason," and "because of."

3. Logical organization – Your essay should be divided into paragraphs, which have been set out in an organized manner. Each body paragraph should contain a point that supports your main idea.

You should also include a conclusion that sums up the essay.

The scorer reading your essay looks for logical paragraph divisions, as well as for linking words and phrases which indicate that a new paragraph is beginning.

4. Writing conventions – Your essay should be grammatically accurate and punctuated correctly. Your spelling should also be correct.

5. Syntactic complexity – You should write long and developed sentences that demonstrate a variety of sentence patterns. You should avoid repeatedly beginning your sentences in the same way, such as "I think that."

The scorer reading your essay will look for a variety of sentence patterns.

6. <u>Appropriate tone and style</u> – Your essay needs to address the concerns of your target audience.

You need to be sure that you have used the correct word choice and style in order to achieve this purpose.

Generally speaking, the tone of your expository essay should be formal, while the tone of your personal experience essay should be expressive.

# How to Avoid Common Essay Errors and Raise Your Score

In the previous section, we talked about the characteristics of a well-written essay.

However, you may also wonder which aspects of an essay would be scored poorly by the person who is evaluating your written work.

These errors most commonly cause students to receive a low score on the CBEST essay:

1. The essay fails to express a clear point of view or provides a viewpoint that cannot be logically supported.

   *Tip:* You can avoid this error by giving a clear thesis statement in the first paragraph of your essay.

2. The essay is written in a tone and style that is not suitable for the audience.

   *Tip:* Using the correct tone and style involves avoiding slang expressions in your writing. Examples of slang language are words like "awesome" or "guy."

3. The reasons or examples provided in the essay are flawed because they do not support the student's main point.

   *Tip:* Be sure that your reasons and examples are closely related to your main idea and to the essay topic. For instance, if you are asked whether art programs should be supported in schools, and then go on to talk about physical education programs because you believe they are similar to art programs, your reasoning would be flawed.

4. The essay is disorganized and therefore difficult to read and score.

   *Tip:* You can avoid this error by brainstorming your ideas and planning your essay before you begin writing.

5. The essay contains errors in sentence construction or contains only simple or repetitive sentence structures.

   *Tip:* Try to avoid writing every sentence of your essay in the subject-verb-object sentence pattern. In order to avoid this shortcoming, you can begin sentences with words and phrases like "although" or "because of this."

6. The essay does not demonstrate a complex thought process.

   *Tip:* Be sure that you give reasons and examples to express and support your position.

7. The essay contains errors in spelling, grammar, and punctuation.

   *Tip:* If you have weaknesses in these areas, you should pay special attention to Parts 4 and 5 of this study guide.

# PART 2 – WRITING THE CBEST EXPOSITORY ESSAY

## CBEST Expository Essay Structure

Most teachers agree that the best CBEST expository essays follow a four to five paragraph format. This format will help to insure that your essay is well-organized.

This format also helps you write longer and more developed essays that will contain 300 to 450 words.

The five paragraph essay is organized as follows:

Paragraph 1 – This paragraph is the introduction to your essay. It should include a thesis statement that clearly indicates your main idea. It can also give the reader an overview of your supporting points.

Paragraph 2 – The second paragraph is where you elaborate on your first supporting point. It is normally recommended that you state your strongest and most persuasive point in this paragraph.

Paragraph 3 – You should elaborate on your main idea in the third paragraph by providing a second supporting point.

Paragraph 4 – You should mention your third supporting point in the fourth paragraph. This can be the supporting point that you feel to be the weakest.

9

Paragraph 5 – In the fifth and final paragraph of the essay, you should make your conclusion. The conclusion can sum up your position or leave the reader with an interesting anecdote or example to consider.

# Creating Effective Thesis Statements

## What is a thesis statement?

A thesis statement is a sentence that asserts the main idea of your essay.

For CBEST expository essays, it is recommended to place the thesis statement in the first sentence of the first paragraph of your essay.

This will make your position on the topic clear and will also create a strong impact as the scorer begins to read your essay.

Most expository essays on the CBEST will be on debatable or contentious topics.

You will not need to write about both sides of the argument for the given topic.

You only need to state which side of the argument you support and give reasons for your viewpoint.

## Write it early

It is important to draft your thesis statement early in the writing process so that your writing has focus. However, be prepared to go back and edit your thesis statement after you have finished the main body of your essay.

## Keep it focused

Remember that the best thesis statements are those that serve to narrow the focus of the essay and control the flow ideas within it.

As such, a thesis statement should not be too general or vague.

For the CBEST essay, it is recommended to begin your sentence with an identifying phrase, such as "I think that" or "I agree that."

*Bearing these tips in mind, you should now complete the thesis statement exercise on the following pages.*

# Thesis Statement – Exercise

*Now look at our essay topic below and write a focused thesis statement.*

Most Americans have access to computers and cell phones on a daily basis, making email and text messaging extremely popular. While some people argue that email and texting are now the most convenient forms of personal communication, others believe that electronic communication technology is often used inappropriately. Write an essay for an audience of educated adults in which you take a position on this topic. Be sure to provide reasons and examples to support your viewpoint.

**Your thesis statement:**

# Thesis Statement – Answer to Exercise

**Suggested answer:**

I agree with the assertion that electronic communication technologies such as email and social media platforms are sometimes used inappropriately.

**Analysis:**

- The thesis statement is clear since it indicates the student's point of view on the topic.

- The student has also identified the sentence as a thesis statement by beginning with the phrase "I agree with the assertion that."

- The above sentence is also an excellent example of a thesis statement since the student focuses his response. The response focuses on email and social media platforms, stating that these media forms are sometimes used inappropriately.

# Writing the Introduction

<u>What is the purpose of the introduction?</u>

The purpose of your introduction is to give a brief statement of your point of view and to provide an overview of your supporting points.

<u>What can I include in my introduction?</u>

You can include a vivid example, an interesting fact, a paradoxical statement, or supporting points in your introduction.

<u>When should I write the introduction?</u>

Although it is advisable to write your thesis statement before beginning your main body, you can often go back and write the remainder of the introduction after you have finished the body paragraphs and conclusion. That is because sometimes it is easier to introduce your essay after you have already written it and developed your points.

<u>What is the structure of the introduction?</u>

The "Assertion + Reason" Structure – A good structure for the introduction is to think of it in terms of an assertion plus a reason or explanation. This structure is better than just giving your assertion or opinion on its own because your explanation indicates the direction that your writing is going to take.

In addition, the "assertion + reason" structure will result in an introduction that contains more words and which is usually richer grammatically and structurally.

The scorer will assess these grammatical and structural aspects of your thesis statement.

Remember that the introduction announces your main idea and supporting points, while your main body develops them.

# Writing the Introduction – Exercise

*Look at our previous essay topic again and write an introduction of 50 to 75 words. Remember to include your thesis statement at the beginning of your introduction. A sample answer is provided on the following page.*

> Most Americans have access to computers and cell phones on a daily basis, making email and text messaging extremely popular. While some people argue that email and texting are now the most convenient forms of personal communication, others believe that electronic communication technology is often used inappropriately. Write an essay for an audience of educated adults in which you take a position on this topic. Be sure to provide reasons and examples to support your viewpoint.

**Your introduction:**

# Writing the Introduction – Answer

**Suggested answer:**

I agree with the assertion that electronic communication technologies such as email and social media platforms are sometimes used inappropriately. Modern forms of communication such as electronic mail and SMS messaging can cause problems with personal relationships because of three main shortcomings with these media: their impersonal nature, their inability to capture tone and sarcasm, and their easy accessibility at times of anger.

**Analysis:**

The second sentence of the introduction follows the "assertion + reason" structure.

The assertion is that "Modern forms of communication such as electronic mail and SMS messaging can cause problems with personal relationships."

The reasons are "their impersonal nature, their inability to capture tone and sarcasm, and their easy accessibility at times of anger."

The expository essay will be focused because it will have three main body paragraphs, which will discuss each of the reasons given in the introduction.

## Organizing the Main Body

"Expository" means to explain. Therefore, each paragraph of your expository essay should explain and expand on your position on the topic.

Each paragraph of your main body should consist of the following elements:

1. A topic sentence which concisely states the supporting point that you are going to discuss in the paragraph.

2. Well-written and complex sentences that elaborate on your supporting points through reasons and examples.

3. The use of subordination and linking words in order to create a variety of different types of sentence construction. If you are unsure about how to subordinate sentences, you may now wish to turn your attention to Part 5 of the study guide before proceeding.

You may wish to write the body of the paragraph before writing your topic sentence for it.

That is because sometimes it is easier to sum up the main point of the paragraph after you have written it.

For this reason, we will next look at the elaboration of supporting points and writing the main body sentences, before turning our attention to topic sentences.

# Elaboration in the Body Paragraphs

How long should each body paragraph be?

For a five paragraph essay, each body paragraph can be approximately 60 to 100 words.

What is an elaborating idea?

Elaborating ideas include both explanations and examples. Providing clear examples to support your points is extremely important.

Each of your main body paragraphs should contain an example that supports your line of argument.

You should elaborate on and explain your example in order to make your essay easy to read and follow.

How do elaborating ideas help to raise my CBEST score?

Elaboration lengthens your essay and gives you more opportunities to demonstrate higher-level grammar and complex sentence construction.

How many elaborating ideas should I have in each paragraph?

You should provide two or three elaborating ideas for each body paragraph.

<u>How do I link my elaborating ideas to one another?</u>

You should seamlessly link your elaborating points together to make a coherent paragraph.

This is the function of linking words and subordination, which we will see in Part 5 of the study guide.

<u>How do I come up with elaborating ideas for each supporting point?</u>

Perhaps the best way to elaborate on your supporting points is to take each of the supporting points that you are going to talk about in your main body paragraphs, place them as headings on a piece of scratch paper, and make a list of examples and explanations under each heading.

*We will have a look at how to do this in the following exercise.*

## Elaboration of Supporting Points – Exercise

Let's turn our attention to our sample essay on email and text communication.

Here is the introduction again for ease of reference:

> I agree with the assertion that electronic communication technologies such as email and social media platforms are sometimes used inappropriately. Modern forms of communication such as electronic mail and SMS messaging can cause problems with personal relationships because of three main shortcomings with these media: their impersonal nature, their inability to capture tone and sarcasm, and their easy accessibility at times of anger.

This will be a five paragraph essay, so in your first body paragraph you need to elaborate on the impersonal nature of electronic communication. Your second body paragraph will elaborate on how emails and texts cannot convey tone and sarcasm.

The third paragraph will talk about the danger of having an accessible messaging service during times of high emotion.

*Exercise – Now try to make a list of the ideas you are going to use as elaboration for each of your main body paragraphs. Sample responses are on the following page.*

**Elaboration – Body Paragraph 1:**

**Elaboration – Body Paragraph 2:**

**Elaboration – Body Paragraph 3:**

# Elaboration of Supporting Points – Answer to Exercise

## Elaboration – Body Paragraph 1:

Elaborate on the impersonal nature of electronic communication

- Email is practical, but not always appropriate. Example: informing someone about a death

- No human contact – can be seen as cold or shallow – not like talking on phone or in person

## Elaboration – Body Paragraph 2:

Emails and texts cannot convey tone and sarcasm

- It is possible for sarcastic comments to be taken literally

- Message clear to sender, but tone of emotion is conveyed by voice

- Without tone, may come across as demanding, indifferent, etc.

## Elaboration – Body Paragraph 3:

The danger of having an accessible messaging service during times of high emotion

- Examples: breaking up with someone by text; firing someone by email

- Easy to send a message quickly when angry – can hurt relationships – waiting and thinking requires self-control & discipline

## Writing the Main Body Paragraphs – Exercise

We had a look at brainstorming ideas for your main body paragraphs in the previous section of this study guide.

We will now focus on the ideas we developed in that section and write the paragraphs of the main body of our essay.

Within each exercise, we reproduce our list of elaborating points for the body paragraphs for ease of reference.

If you have difficulties with grammar, this would be a good point to have a look at the CBEST English Grammar Review section in Part 4 of this study guide.

*Now write the sentences for main body paragraphs for your expository essay, excluding the topic sentences. Some words from the basic sentence structure of the sample response are provided in order to guide you. Refer to the lists above each exercise to help you. Write each new sentence in the order of the points provided*

## Main Body Paragraph 1:

Elaborate on the impersonal nature of electronic communication

- Email is practical, but not always appropriate. Example: informing someone about a death

- No human contact – can be seen as cold or shallow – not like talking on phone or in person

*Sentence 1*: Although email may be practical for . . . , electronic messaging would be remarkably inappropriate for . . .

*Sentence 2*: There is no direct human contact in . . . , and during times of loss or tragedy, human warmth . . .

## Main Body Paragraph 2:

Emails and texts cannot convey tone and sarcasm

- It is possible for sarcastic comments to be taken literally

- Message clear to sender, but tone of emotion is conveyed by voice

- Without tone, may come across as demanding, indifferent, etc.

*Sentence 1*: For instance, it might be possible . . . of a sarcastic email message to . . .

*Sentence 2*: The tone of . . . may seem abundantly clear to . . . , but sarcastic or ironically humorous utterances can only . . .

*Sentence 3*: Without . . . , certain phrases in an email may . . .

**Main Body Paragraph 3:**

The danger of having an accessible messaging service during times of high emotion

- Examples: breaking up with someone by text; firing someone by email

- Easy to send a message quickly when angry – can hurt relationships – waiting and thinking requires self-control & discipline

*Sentence 1*: In this day and age, we have heard stories not only of . . . , but also of employers who . . .

*Sentence 2*: Unless the writer of the message has  . . . before . . . , he or she might send a regrettable message that can . . .

# Suggested Answers – Main Body Paragraphs

**Sample Body Paragraph 1 (excluding topic sentence):**

Although email may be practical for conveying straightforward information or facts, electronic messaging would be remarkably inappropriate for events like announcing a death. There is no direct human contact in emails and texts, and during times of loss or tragedy, human warmth and depth of emotion can only truly be conveyed through a phone call, or better still, by talking face to face.

**Sample Body Paragraph 2 (excluding topic sentence):**

For instance, it might be possible for the recipient of a sarcastic email message to take its contents literally. The tone of the message may seem abundantly clear to the person who sent it, but sarcastic or ironically humorous utterances can only really be communicated in speech through the tone and inflection of the voice. Without the aid of tone and inflection, certain phrases in an email may come across as demanding, indifferent, or rude.

**Sample Body Paragraph 3 (excluding topic sentence):**

In this day and age, we have heard stories not only of personal break ups that have been conducted by text, but also of employers who fire their staff by email message. Unless the writer of the message has the discipline and self-control to give him or herself a period of reasoned contemplation before sending the communication, he or she might send a regrettable message that can cause irretrievable damage to a relationship.

# Writing Clear and Concise Topic Sentences

## Why are topic sentences important?

As the scorer reads each new paragraph of your CBEST essays, he or she will look for new ideas by searching for words and phrases that you have not used previously in your writing.

Each topic sentence can therefore be a paraphrase, *but should not repeat word for word*, the supporting points in your introduction.

## What is the purpose of a topic sentence?

You can think of the topic sentence as a summary of the content of a main body paragraph. The topic sentence serves two purposes.

First of all, it gives an overview of the content of the paragraph because it announces the topic that you are going to discuss.

Secondly, the topic sentence links back to the introduction since it is an elaboration of one of the supporting points that you have already cited at the beginning of the essay.

In this way, clear and concise topic sentences give your essay cohesion and coherence.

### Is a topic sentence general or specific in its focus?

While the topic sentence is more specific than the introduction to the essay, the topic sentence should be more general than the elaboration that you are going to make in the paragraph.

In other words, each main body paragraph should move from the more general supporting point that you mention in your topic sentence to the specific points that you raise in your elaboration.

### How do I avoid repeating myself?

Remember that although your topic sentences point back to the introduction, you need to avoid using the exact same wording in your topic sentences as in your introduction.

For instance, if you refer to the "impersonal nature of electronic communication" in your introduction, your topic sentence should word this idea differently.

In this case, the phrase "impersonal nature of electronic communication" could be paraphrased by stating: "There is no direct human contact in email."

### Where should a topic sentence be placed within the paragraph?

The most common position for the topic sentence is the first sentence of the paragraph.

In longer essays, it is possible to put a topic sentence as the second sentence of a paragraph if the paragraph's first sentence is transitional.

You can also delay the topic sentence until the end of the paragraph for emphasis, although for the sake of clarity, this is not recommended.

For the CBEST essay, you should plan to write three or four main body paragraphs, each of which have a topic sentence as their first sentence.

# Topic Sentences – Exercise

Let's turn our attention to writing topic sentences for the main body paragraphs of our essay on email and text communication.

The topic sentence for your first body paragraph will mention the impersonal nature of electronic communication.

Your topic sentence for the second body paragraph will mention how the tone of emails and texts can be misunderstood.

The topic sentence of your third paragraph will talk about the danger of having a quick messaging service at hand when you are angry.

*Exercise – Now try to write topic sentences for each of your main body paragraphs. Remember that the topic sentence needs to be specific for each supporting point, but general enough to introduce the paragraph as a whole. You may wish to refer back to what you have written thus far on the essay topic. Sample responses are provided on the next page.*

**Topic Sentence 1:**


**Topic Sentence 2:**


**Topic Sentence 3:**

# Topic Sentences – Answer to Exercise

*Here are possible topic sentences for the three main body paragraphs.*

**Topic Sentence 1:**

Depending upon the context, the recipient of an email or text message may consider this mode of communication to be insensitive or uncaring.

**Analysis:**

The phrase "their impersonal nature" from the introduction has been re-worded as "insensitive or uncaring."

**Topic Sentence 2:**

A further problem with emails and texts is that they do not always accurately express the tone which the writer has intended.

**Analysis:**

The idea of "their inability to capture tone and sarcasm" from the introduction has been paraphrased as "they do not always accurately express the tone which the writer has intended."

**Topic Sentence 3:**

The danger of having an accessible messaging service readily at hand during times of high emotion is another insidious problem with electronic media.

**Analysis:**

The phrase "their easy accessibility at times of anger" from the introduction has been expressed here as "readily at hand during times of high emotion."

Also note that the words "further" from topic sentence 2 and "another" from topic sentence 3 improve the flow of the essay by signaling that new ideas are being introduced in these paragraphs.

# Writing the Conclusion

Conclusions for CBEST essays can consist of as few as two sentences, provided that the sentences are cohesive, coherent, and well-constructed. You may want to reiterate certain concepts in the conclusion. However, you should avoid repeating word for word what you have already written. That is to say that your conclusion can echo your introduction, but you should not repeat the exact phrases you have already used at the start of your essay or in the body paragraphs.

The final sentence of your conclusion can also be used to give advice or to make a prediction about the future. This will give a forward-looking aspect to your essay and will help your writing to end on a strong note.

# Writing the Conclusion – Exercise

*Look at the underlined words from the introduction to the essay below.*

*Then look at the sample conclusion and identify the words which paraphrase these concepts.*

*Finally, circle the useful phrases that are used in the sample conclusion.*

## Introduction:

I agree with the assertion that electronic communication technologies such as email and social media platforms are sometimes used inappropriately. Modern forms of communication such as electronic mail and SMS messaging can cause problems with personal relationships because of three main shortcomings with these media: their <u>impersonal nature</u>, their <u>inability to capture tone and sarcasm</u>, and their <u>easy accessibility at times of anger</u>.

## Conclusion:

While email and texts may therefore be useful for certain aspects of our daily lives, these communication methods need to be handled with care in some situations, particularly when they could be seen as insensitive, when it is possible that the recipient might misinterpret the meaning, or when composed at times of personal agitation or stress. The writer of the message should use judgment and common sense in order to avoid the ill feelings that may be caused to the recipient in these cases.

| Original wording in the introduction: | Paraphrasing in the conclusion: |
|---|---|
| impersonal nature | |
| inability to capture tone and sarcasm | |
| easy accessibility at times of anger | |

**Useful phrases in the conclusion:**

**What advice or prediction is made in the conclusion?**

# Writing the Conclusion – Answer

| Original wording in the introduction: | Paraphrasing in the conclusion: |
|---|---|
| impersonal nature | could be seen as insensitive |
| inability to capture tone and sarcasm | the recipient might misinterpret the meaning |
| easy accessibility at times of anger | composed at times of personal agitation or stress |

**Useful phrases in the conclusion:**

while

particularly

when

in order to

**What advice or prediction is made in the conclusion?**

The following piece of advice is given in the last sentence of the conclusion to the essay: The writer of the message should use judgment and common sense in order to avoid the ill feelings that may be caused to the recipient in these cases.

# SAMPLE EXPOSITORY ESSAY – MODEL ESSAY 1

*We reproduce here in full our sample essay, which we have worked on throughout the previous sections of this study guide.*

**Sample Essay 1:**

I agree with the assertion that electronic communication technologies such as email and social media platforms are sometimes used inappropriately. Modern forms of communication such as electronic mail and SMS messaging can cause problems with personal relationships because of three main shortcomings with these media: their impersonal nature, their inability to capture tone and sarcasm, and their easy accessibility at times of anger.

Depending upon the context, the recipient of an email or text message may consider this mode of communication to be insensitive or uncaring. Although email may be practical for conveying straightforward information or facts, electronic messaging would be remarkably inappropriate for events like announcing a death. There is no direct human contact in emails and texts, and during times of loss or tragedy, human warmth and depth of emotion can only truly be conveyed through a phone call, or better still, by talking face to face.

A further problem with emails and texts is that they do not always accurately express the tone which the writer has intended. For instance, it might be possible for the recipient of a sarcastic email message to take its contents literally. The tone of the message may seem abundantly clear to the person who sent it, but sarcastic or ironically humorous utterances can only really be communicated in speech through the tone and inflection of the voice. Without the aid of tone and inflection, certain phrases in an email may come across as demanding, indifferent, or rude.

The danger of having an accessible messaging service readily at hand during times of high emotion is another insidious problem with electronic media. In this day and age, we have heard stories not only of personal break ups that have been conducted by text, but also of employers who fire their staff by email message. Unless the writer of the message has the discipline and self-control to give him or herself a period of reasoned contemplation before sending the communication, he or she might send a regrettable message that can cause irretrievable damage to a relationship.

While email and texts may therefore be useful for certain aspects of our daily lives, these communication methods need to be handled with care in some situations, particularly when they could be seen as insensitive, when it is possible that the recipient might misinterpret the meaning, or when composed at times of personal agitation or stress. The writer of the message should use judgment and common sense in order to avoid the ill feelings that may be caused to the recipient in these cases.

*In the next part of the study guide, we include two additional expository essays. You should analyze and study the format and language usage in each expository essay before proceeding to the section on writing the personal experience essay.*

## SAMPLE EXPOSITORY ESSAY – MODEL ESSAY 2

Thomas Edison once stated: "Restlessness and discontent are the first necessities of progress." Please state whether you agree or disagree with this assertion, giving compelling reasons and examples to support your argument. Your essay should be written for an audience of educated adults.

Like Thomas Edison, I support the view that restlessness and discontent are the first necessities of progress. This simple assertion holds true both on the societal and personal levels.

It is irrefutable that restlessness can lead to progress within society. During the pre-revolutionary period in American history, for example, the settlers in the American colonies became very restless with the way that English law was treating them. This restlessness led to the American Revolutionary War, which witnessed the birth of a myriad of personal and social liberties that American citizens still enjoy today.

In addition, great innovations have come about and continue to come about because of discontent or dissatisfaction with the current state of affairs. Because of this basic principle, many great inventions have been created and many discoveries have occurred. In the nineteenth century, for instance, Louis Braille had an accident at three years of age which caused him to become blind. When he became older, Braille realized that the vast intellectual world of thought and ideas would be closed to him forever unless he devised a system whereby the blind could read. It was this dissatisfaction that led Braille to create the system of type that sight-impaired people around the world utilize today.

Likewise, restlessness and discontent on an individual level can also lead to personal progress. I myself have had life experiences that illustrate this principle. Having worked in an office for many years as an accountant, I realized that I was restless with and discontent in this line of work. This dissatisfaction led me to a journey of self-discovery, culminating in my decision to return to college as a mature student in order to study education.

That is not to say that satisfaction and contentment, whether on a personal or social level, are not to be sought-after. But while satisfaction and contentment can be admirable characteristics in certain ways, these states of mind rarely lead to the social or personal struggles that are necessary in order for change or innovation to occur.

## ANALYSIS OF MODEL ESSAY 2:

1. Clear central idea – the writer expresses his central idea clearly in the opening paragraph of the essay when he states: "I support the view that restlessness and discontent are the first necessities of progress [. . . which] holds true both on the societal and personal levels."

2. Well-supported – the essay is well-supported with meaningful explanations and examples. The writer gives examples from Louise Braille's life and the American Revolutionary War, as well as a description of a personal experience to illustrate his viewpoint.

3. Logical organization – the essay is structured very well and is easy to follow and read. The arguments in support of the social implications of the assertion are stated in paragraphs 2 and 3, while the personal implications of the assertion are stated in paragraph 4.

4. Writing conventions – the student has utilized correct grammar, spelling, and punctuation. The essay is also organized into meaningful paragraphs, each of which centers around a key example or point.

5. Syntactic complexity – the structure of the sentences in this essay is very complex. The writer uses linking words and phrases such as

when, in addition, during, and likewise to achieve this effect.

Please study the underlined words and phrases in the essay and

pay attention to how they are being used. If you are unsure of how

to construct sentences in this way, please refer to Part 5 of this

study guide.

6. Appropriate tone and style – the writer expresses his points of view

in a formal, academic way. The level of vocabulary he uses

demonstrates that he is writing to an audience of educated adults.

# SAMPLE EXPOSITORY ESSAY – MODEL ESSAY 3

> "Money can't buy happiness."  Please comment on this statement, giving compelling reasons and examples. Your essay should be written for an audience of educated adults.

I believe in the general concept that money can't buy happiness. Yet, I would also like to add that it is an equally valid point that having a sufficient amount of money can save a person from experiencing a great deal of agony.

Philosophically speaking, happiness and contentment are inner states of mind that are not connected to the tangible world of material existence. Buddhist monks take vows of poverty, and yet they are quite possibly the most content human beings that one could ever encounter. Further, there are known cases of people who have endured unspeakable hardships and nevertheless have continued to have faith in humankind. The *Diary of Anne Frank* is an elucidating example in this case.  When reading the writings of this young Jewish girl, one can plainly see that Anne managed to maintain a cheerful outlook throughout her ordeal, in spite of the persecution and hardships she experienced daily while hiding from Nazi soldiers during the Second World War.

Conversely, money itself can be the cause of profound sadness for many people. Nearly every week one can read stories in the media about family feuds over inheritances or lottery winners who find that their friends have turned against them after failing to be given sizeable monetary gifts. What is more, some wealthy people are too preoccupied with increasing their fortunes to stop and enjoy the fruits of their labors by taking a well-deserved vacation or simply spending time relaxing with their families.

It is worth mentioning though, that while money can't buy happiness *per se*, it can alleviate many sources of suffering. Consider, for instance, the person who does not have adequate medical care because he or she cannot afford it. In this case, happiness could be achieved by having ample financial resources to return the person to full health. Of course, even more compelling is the example of children around the globe who must endure the effects of poverty on a daily basis.

Indeed, it seems an existential luxury to engage in philosophical musings over the elusive state of "happiness" when people in many countries around the world will wake up today without the sufficient food, medicine, and drinking water needed for mere survival.

## ANALYSIS OF MODEL ESSAY 3:

1. Clear central idea – the writer expresses her central idea clearly in the opening paragraph of the essay when she states: "I believe in the general concept that money can't buy happiness. Yet, I would also like to add that it is an equally valid point that having a sufficient amount of money can save a person from experiencing a great deal of agony." From this sentence, the reader can see that the writer primarily agrees with the essay theme, although she will go on to express certain reservations.

2. Well-supported – the essay is well-supported with meaningful explanations and examples. The writer cites the examples of Buddhist monks, Anne Frank, the discontent of the wealthy, and world poverty to support her position.

3. Logical organization – the essay is structured very well and is easy to follow and read. The arguments in support of the primary assertion are stated in paragraphs 2 and 3, while the writer's reservations are stated in paragraphs 4 and 5.

4. Writing conventions – the student has utilized correct grammar, spelling, and punctuation. The essay is also organized into meaningful paragraphs, each of which focuses on a key point.

5. Syntactic complexity – the structure of the sentences in this essay is very complex.  The writer uses linking words such as however, nevertheless, for example, while, and however to achieve this effect.  You should again study and analyze the underlined words and phrases in this essay.

6. Appropriate tone and style – the writer expresses her opinion in a clear and assertive way, but she also shows that she can contemplate other viewpoints by using the phrases:  it is worth mentioning, I would also like to add that, and it seems.

# PART 3 – WRITING THE PERSONAL EXPERIENCE ESSAY

## CBEST Personal Experience Essay Structure

As stated at the beginning of this study guide, the purpose of the CBEST personal experience essay is to allow you to express yourself in your writing.

However, that is not to say that the personal experience essay should lack structure or that it can be poorly written.

Even though the structure of the personal experience essay is much freer than that of the expository essay, you may want to follow the organization pattern recommended below.

Paragraph 1

In the first paragraph of the personal experience essay, you should describe and make clear which life event you are going to talk about.

For example, if you are going to talk about a car accident that you were involved in, you should mention that you had an accident.

In other words, you should avoid making a vague statement like "My life was affected by an unfortunate event in my childhood."

The scorer will appreciate clarity as he or she gets focused on your topic at the beginning of your piece.

## The body paragraphs

There is no set number of paragraphs that you should use in the personal experience piece.

You could have as few as two and as many as five body paragraphs.

The important point is to be sure that you have expressed yourself clearly and that you have recounted your personal experience more or less completely.

You may find it useful to write about your story chronologically in order to keep your main body paragraphs organized.

## The final paragraph

In the last paragraph of your personal response piece, you should bring your personal story to a close.

You can do this by reiterating the reason why the life event was such a significant one for you.

# CBEST Personal Experience Essay Tips

Keep it personal

Remember that task 2 is a personal piece. As such, it can and should use first-person pronouns ("I," "me," "my," and "myself,") since you will be recounting a personal experience.

Tone and style

The tone of the personal experience piece will be less formal that that of the expository piece.

Keep it organized

The useful phrases in the next section of the study guide will help you to organize your personal experience piece and keep it focused.

First of all, you should study the list of words provided on the next page. You should then analyze how these phrases are used in the sample personal experience essays that follow the list of phrases.

# Useful Phrases for the Personal Experience Essay

Actions

I began to

I coped by

I embarked upon

Without realizing it, I (did something).

Decisions

I considered (doing something).

I decided to (do something).

I reacted by (doing something).

Discoveries

I came to the conclusion that

I came to the realization that

I discovered that

I found that

I heard that

I realized that

I was informed that

## Feelings

The despair I felt

The happiness I felt

The joy I felt

I was distressed when

I was elated when

Much to my delight,

Much to my despair,

## Influences

I grew up with

I was influenced by

I was raised to

It was a decisive factor in

He / She demonstrated to me that

The support / love / care / attention I received was invaluable / priceless.

## Outcomes

I certainly would have (done something) if I had (known something).

In the end,

It ultimately led to

This instinct remained with me

<u>Thoughts</u>

I contemplated (doing something).

I thought about

I thought that

I mused upon

My thoughts were

*Now have a look at the sample personal experience essays that follow and study the useful phrases in each one.*

# SAMPLE PERSONAL EXPERIENCE ESSAY – MODEL ESSAY 4

It is often said that every cloud has a silver lining. Describe a difficult situation that you faced in your personal or professional life and explain how you ultimately worked out the problem to your advantage.

When I received word that my application for college had not been accepted, I thought life as I knew it was going to end. "How could life be so unjust?" I mused, as I saw the upcoming academic year stretch out in front of me like a deserted highway. Little did I know that this delay in my academic path would ultimately lead to something truly wonderful.

If I had realized that a simple administrative error on my part was going to delay my studies, I certainly would have been more careful in submitting the necessary forms. I was so self-assured that I was going to be accepted that I had not even bothered to look for work. Nor had I taken into account where I was going to live. Hence, I embarked upon what could have been a year of self-doubt and recrimination.

However, instead of sinking into a quagmire of depression, I decided to take that year as an opportunity to rethink my options. I began to ask myself some hard questions. Did I really want to study in the degree program I had chosen?  How committed was I to the idea of financing my own higher education?

I spent weeks scouring the internet for various degree programs and requested a plethora of course catalogues from institutions of higher learning in other states.  I then narrowed down my options to nine or ten different colleges.

Invigorated by a new sense of optimism, I requested financial aid and scholarship information from the colleges I had chosen.  In the end, three colleges looked the most promising, so I decided to submit applications for admissions, as well as scholarship applications to those places.

Then came the really tough part: waiting for a response.  Much to my delight, I was accepted for study at a university in California.  I was informed that I would receive a decision about my scholarship application within two months.

The joy I felt when I found out that I had received a full scholarship more than outstripped the agony I had experienced less than a year earlier. Had I not had that setback, I never would have decided to pursue a degree in education.

## ANALYSIS OF MODEL ESSAY 4:

1. Clear central idea – the writer expresses his central idea clearly in the opening sentence of the essay when he writes: "When I received word that my application for college had not been accepted, I thought life as I knew it was going to end." Therefore, the examiner can clearly see from the beginning which personal experience the candidate is going to discuss.

2. Well-supported – the essay is well-supported with meaningful explanations and examples. The writer vividly describes his disappointment, as well as the steps he took to overcome his difficulties.

3. Logical organization – the essay is structured very well and is easy to follow and read. The student achieves excellent organization by describing events in chronological order.

4. Writing conventions – the student has utilized correct grammar, spelling, and punctuation. In particular, please notice how to punctuate dialogue and quotations. Remember that punctuation for dialogue should be included within the quotation marks.

5. Syntactic complexity – the structure of the sentences in this essay is very complex. The writer uses linking words and phrases such as

if, hence, and nor.  The student also begins sentences with past participle phrases.  Please see Part 5 of this study guide for advice on how to write sentences in this way.

6.  Appropriate tone and style – the writer recounts his life event in an expressive way.  Please study the underlined phrases that he uses, which are from the list of useful phrases for the personal experience essay on the previous pages.

## SAMPLE PERSONAL EXPERIENCE ESSAY – MODEL ESSAY 5

Explain what led to your decision to become a teacher. Please support your explanation with reasons and examples. Your essay should be written for an audience of educated adults.

Like many of my colleagues who are <u>about to embark on</u> a career in teaching, <u>I was positively influenced by</u> a teacher who helped me through some difficult personal struggles. <u>The support and concern that</u> this teacher gave me were a major factor in my own decision to enter the teaching profession.

Having had very prominent buck teeth until undergoing orthodontic work in my late teens, I was dubbed "Bugs Bunny" by my classmates in elementary school. Already an awkward and shy youngster, <u>I found that</u> this appellation, although perhaps meant in only jest, exacerbated my lack of self-confidence. <u>I coped with</u> the problem the best I could have at that age: by retreating into my own world of books and reading.

Fortunately, I had one close friend throughout grades 3, 4, and 5. She shared my affinity with reading, and we often exchanged books with each other during summer vacations. <u>Without even realizing it</u>, I was quickly becoming a very proficient reader at a young age.  Yet, while improving my reading skill, this habit did little for my self-confidence.

Upon returning to school at the beginning of the sixth grade, my entire self-concept began to change.  When I found out that I would be having Mrs. Shelley as my home room and reading teacher, I was absolutely elated. I had heard so many nice things about her and her classes, and she always had a warm smile and time to talk to everyone she met.

Mrs. Shelley started a reading competition for the class that year.  Each student had a path on the wall to chart his or her progress.  Construction-paper cut-outs of footprints were placed on each student's path each week to represent the number of books that the student had read. Every week, I was reading two or three books, and soon Mrs. Shelley had to prepare another path for me as my first one had become full.  My classmates, seeing that my progress was more rapid than theirs, began to call me names in class.  Mrs. Shelley then stepped in and saw to it that the taunts of geek, nerd, and brainer were quickly silenced.

Moreover, Mrs. Shelly often complimented me in private after class about my reading skills.  Her kindness and sincerity demonstrated to me at an early age the true essence of being a good teacher.  Soon my classmates' views of me just didn't matter anymore.  <u>I had found</u> something that was important to me: the desire to help other people the way that Mrs. Shelley had helped me. <u>This impulse remained with me</u> throughout middle school and high school, and <u>it was the decisive factor in</u> my own decision to become a teacher.

## ANALYSIS OF SAMPLE MODEL 5:

1. Clear central idea – the writer expresses the main idea in the opening sentence of the essay when she states: "Like many of my colleagues who are about to embark on a career in teaching, I was positively influenced by a teacher who helped me through some difficult personal struggles."

2. Well-supported – the essay is well-supported with expressive and personal examples. The writer discusses how she dealt with her derisive nickname, and how this went on to help her become a good reader and ultimately a teacher herself.

3. Logical organization – the essay is structured very well and is easy to follow and read. Like model essay 4, the writer recounts events in chronological order.

4. Writing conventions – the student has utilized correct grammar, spelling, punctuation, and paragraphing.

5. Syntactic complexity – the structure of the sentences in this essay is very complex. The writer uses subordination and linking words such as like, although, fortunately, and however to achieve this effect.

6. Appropriate tone and style – the writer recounts her experience in an extremely expressive way. She achieves this effect by using words and phrases from the list that we have seen previously.

*Use of the following grammatical conventions is necessary for an effective essay. Please read the following pages carefully, and then have another look at how these conventions are used in the sample essays provided previously in study guide.*

## Using Correct Grammar and Punctuation

Mechanical conventions are the rules of grammar and punctuation that are

necessary in order to write accurately and correctly.

This section covers some of the basic rules of grammar, punctuation, and

sentence construction that are assessed in your CBEST essays.

## Avoiding Misplaced Modifiers

Modifiers are descriptive phrases. The modifier should always be placed directly before or after the noun to which it relates.

Now look at the examples.

CORRECT: Like Montana, Wyoming is not very densely populated.

INCORRECT: Like Montana, there isn't a large population in Wyoming.

The phrase "like Montana" is an adjectival phrase that modifies the noun

"Wyoming."

Therefore, "Wyoming" must come directly after the comma.

Here are two more examples:

CORRECT: While waiting at the bus stop, a senior citizen was mugged.

INCORRECT: While waiting at the bus stop, a mugging took place.

The adverbial phrase "*while waiting at the bus stop*" modifies the noun phrase "a senior citizen," so this noun phrase needs to come after the adverbial phrase.

**Negative Inversion**

When a sentence begins with a negative phrase [no sooner, not only, never, etc.], the present perfect tense [have + past participle] must be used.

CORRECT: Never in my life have I seen such a beautiful sight.

INCORRECT: Never in my life I have seen such a beautiful sight.

This sentence is an example of the inverted sentence structure.

Note that the auxiliary verb "have" must be placed *in front of* the grammatical subject of the sentence [I].

**Past Participle Phrases**

Past participles are verb forms that are similar to the past simple tense in their form. In other words, past participles usually end in -ed [in cases of regular verbs].

For example: the past participle of the verb "fluster" is "flustered."

CORRECT: Flustered, Shirley failed her driving test.

INCORRECT: Flustered Shirley failed her driving test.

Remember to put the past participle phrase immediately before or after the noun it modifies.

Also remember to use commas before and after the past participle phrase.

**Past Perfect Tense**

The past perfect is often used to express an action which has just recently occurred. It can also be used to show that one action preceded another when a sentence describes two actions.

> When describing two actions, the past perfect is used for the action which happened first. The simple past is used for the subsequent action.

CORRECT: Their adversaries in the southern states, the Confederates, had consolidated and called themselves the Confederate States of America.

INCORRECT: Their adversaries in the southern states, the Confederates, consolidated and had called themselves the Confederate States of America.

In other words, the consolidation occurred first. After this, the states began to call themselves the new name.

> The past perfect is often used with the words "just" and "after," and with the phrase "no sooner . . . than." The auxiliary verb must come before the word "just."

CORRECT: We had just arrived, when she decided to leave.

INCORRECT: We just had arrived, when she decided to leave.

**Pronoun-Antecedent Agreement**

Pronouns are words like the following: he, she, it, they, and them.
An antecedent is a phrase that precedes the pronoun in the sentence.

Pronouns must agree with their antecedents.

Now look at the examples below.

CORRECT: Each student needs to bring his or her identification to the

placement test.

INCORRECT: Each student needs to bring their identification to the

placement test.

The antecedent "each student" is singular, so the singular pronouns "his"

or "her" should follow this antecedent.

**Pronoun Usage – Correct Use of *Its* and *It's***

"Its" is a possessive pronoun, while "it's" is a contraction of "it is".

CORRECT: It's high time you started to study.

INCORRECT: Its high time you started to study.

The sentence could also be stated as follows: It is high time you started to

study.

Since the contracted form of "it is" can be used in the alternative sentence

above, "it's" is the correct form.

CORRECT: A snake sheds its skin at least once a year.

INCORRECT: A snake sheds it's skin at least once a year.

"Its" is a possessive pronoun referring to the snake, so the apostrophe should not be used.

**Pronoun Usage – Correct Use of *Their, There* and *They're***

"Their" is a plural possessive pronoun. "There" is used to describe the location of something. "They're" is a contraction of "they are".

CORRECT: Their house is made of brick and concrete.

INCORRECT: There house is made of brick and concrete.

INCORRECT: They're house is made of brick and concrete.

In this case, "their" is the possessive pronoun explaining to whom the house belongs.

CORRECT: He attended college with his cousins living there in California.

INCORRECT: He attended college with his cousins living their in California.

INCORRECT: He attended college with his cousins living they're in California.

"There" is referring to the state of California in the example above, so it is used to talk about the location.

CORRECT: They're away on vacation at the moment.

INCORRECT: Their away on vacation at the moment.

INCORRECT: There away on vacation at the moment.

The sentence could also be written as follows: They are away on vacation

at the moment.

"They're" is a contraction of "they are," so the apostrophe needs to be

used.

## Pronoun Usage – Avoiding "You" and "Your"

The pronouns "you" and "your" are informal and should generally be
avoided in academic writing when referring to a person in general.

FORMAL: Students should plan in advance if they intend to do well on the

project.

INFORMAL: You should plan in advance if you intend to do well on the

project.

## Pronoun Usage – Demonstrative Pronouns

Demonstrative pronouns include the following words: this, that, these, those

This" is used for a singular item that is nearby. "That" is used for singular

items that are farther away in time or space.

SINGULAR: This book that I have here is really interesting.

PLURAL: That book on the table over there is really interesting.

"These" is used for plural items that are nearby. "Those" is used for plural items that are farther away in time or space.

SINGULAR: These pictures in my purse were taken on our vacation.

PLURAL: Those pictures on the wall were taken on our vacation.

Avoid using "them" instead of "those":

INCORRECT: Them pictures on the wall were taken on our vacation.

**Pronoun Usage – Relative Pronouns**

Relative pronouns include the following: which, that, who, whom, whose

> "Which" and "that" are used to describe things, and "who" and "whom" are used to describe people. "Whose" is used for people or things.

WHICH: Last night, I watched a romantic-comedy movie which was really funny.

THAT: Last night, I watched a romantic-comedy movie that was really funny.

WHO: Susan always remains calm under pressure, unlike Tom, who is always so nervous.

"Who" is used because we are describing the person. This is known as the nominative case.

WHOM: To whom should the report be given?

"Whom" is used because the person is receiving an action, which in this case is receiving the report. This is known as the accusative case.

WHOSE: I went out for lunch with Marta, whose parents are from Costa Rica.

WHOSE: I went out for lunch yesterday at that new restaurant, whose name I don't remember.

Please be sure to look at the section entitled "Restrictive and Non-restrictive Modifiers" for information on how to use punctuation with relative pronouns.

**Punctuation – Avoiding the Parenthetical**

Parentheticals should normally not be used to add extra information to a sentence.

Commas should be used, where possible. Alternatively, two sentences should be written.

CORRECT: Because of drinking beforehand, the driver of the SUV lost control of the vehicle, which overturned on highway and then rolled down the embankment.

CORRECT: The SUV overturned on the highway and then rolled down the embankment after the driver lost control of the vehicle. The accident happened because he had been drinking beforehand.

INCORRECT: The SUV overturned on the highway and then rolled down the embankment after the driver (because of drinking beforehand) lost control of the vehicle.

## Punctuation – Using the Apostrophe for Possessive Forms

Apostrophe placement depends upon whether a word is singular or plural.

For the singular, the apostrophe should be placed before the letter "s."

SINGULAR: Our team's performance was poor at the game last night.

For the plural form, the apostrophe should be placed after the letter "s."

PLURAL: Both teams' performances were poor at the game last night.

Remember that the apostrophe is used in sentences like those above in order to show possession.

Do not use the apostrophe unnecessarily.

INCORRECT: The date's for the events are June 22 and July 5.

INCORRECT: The dates' for the events are June 22 and July 5.

## Punctuation – Using Colons and Semicolons

Colons (:) should be used when giving a list of items. Semicolons (;) should be used to join independent clauses.

COLON: The shop is offering discounts on the following items: DVDs, books, and magazines.

SEMICOLON: I thought I would live in this city forever; then I lost my job.

Please see the section entitled "Punctuation and Independent Clauses" for

more information on joining clauses.

**Punctuation – Using Commas with Dates and Locations**

Commas should be used after the date and year in dates. Commas should also be used after towns and states.

DATES: On July 4, 1776, the Declaration of Independence was signed.

LOCATIONS: Located in Seattle, Washington, the Space Needle is a

major landmark.

**Punctuation – Using Commas for Items in a Series**

When using "and" and "or" for more than two items in a series, be sure to use the comma before the words "and" and "or."

CORRECT: You need to bring a tent, sleeping bag, and flashlight.

INCORRECT: You need to bring a tent, sleeping bag and flashlight.

Notice the use of the comma after the word "bag" and before the word

"and" in the series.

CORRECT: Students can call, write a letter, or send an email.

INCORRECT: Students can call, write a letter or send an email.

Notice the use of the comma after the word "letter" and before the word

"or" in the series.

## Punctuation and Independent Clauses – Avoiding Run-On Sentences

> Run-on sentences are those that use commas to join independent clauses together, instead of correctly using the period.

An independent clause contains a grammatical subject and verb. It therefore can stand alone as its own sentence.

The first word of the independent clause should begin with a capital letter, and the clause should be preceded by a period.

CORRECT: I thought I would live in this city forever. Then I lost my job.

INCORRECT: I thought I would live in this city forever, then I lost my job.

"Then I lost my job" is a complete sentence. It has a grammatical subject (I) and a verb (lost). The independent clause must be preceded by a period, and the first word of the new sentence must begin with a capital letter.

Alternatively, an appropriate conjunction can be used to join the independent clauses:

I thought I would live in this city forever, and then I lost my job.

## Punctuation and Quotation Marks

> Punctuation should be enclosed within the final quotation mark when giving dialogue.

INCORRECT: "I can't believe you bought a new car", Sam remarked.

CORRECT: "I can't believe you bought a new car," Sam remarked.

The word *exclaimed* shows that the exclamation point is needed in the following examples.

INCORRECT: "I can't believe you bought a new car"! Sam exclaimed.

CORRECT: "I can't believe you bought a new car!" Sam exclaimed.

### Restrictive and Non-restrictive Modifiers

> Restrictive modifiers are clauses or phrases that provide essential information that is needed in order to identify the grammatical subject.

Restrictive modifiers should not be preceded by a comma.

Example: My sister who lives in Indianapolis is a good swimmer.

In this case, the speaker has more than one sister, and she is identifying which sister she is talking about by giving the essential information "who lives in Indianapolis."

On the other hand, a non-restrictive modifier is a clause or phrase that provides extra information about a grammatical subject in a sentence. A non-restrictive modifier must be preceded by a comma.

Non-restrictive modifiers are also known as non-essential modifiers.

Example: My sister, who lives in Indianapolis, is a good swimmer.

In this case, the speaker has only one sister. Therefore, the information about her sister's city of residence is not essential in order to identify

which sister she is talking about. So, the words "who lives in Indianapolis"

form a non-restrictive modifier.

## Sentence Fragments

> A sentence fragment is a group of words that does not express a complete train of thought.

CORRECT: I like Christine because she is so nice.

INCORRECT: I like Christine. Because she is so nice.

In the second example, "because she is so nice" is not a complete

thought. This idea needs to be joined with the previous clause in order to

be grammatically correct.

## Subject-Verb Agreement

> Subjects must agree with verbs in number. Be careful with singulars and plurals.

Subject-verb agreement can be confusing when there are intervening

words in a sentence.

CORRECT: The flowers in the pots in the garden grow quickly.

INCORRECT: The flowers in the pots in the garden grows quickly.

The grammatical subject in the above sentence is "flowers," not "garden,"

so the plural form of the verb (*grow*) needs to be used.

CORRECT: Each person in the groups of students needs to pay attention to the instructions.

INCORRECT: Each person in the groups of students need to pay attention to the instructions.

The grammatical subject in the above sentence is "each person," not "students." "Each" is singular and therefore requires the singular form of the verb (*needs*).

*Now try the grammar exercises on the next page.*

# Grammar and Punctuation – Exercises

*Each of the sentences below has problems with grammar and punctuation. Find the errors in the sentences and correct them. You may wish to refer to the advice in the previous section as you do the exercise. The answers are provided on the page following the exercises.*

1) I haven't seen her or her sister. Since they went away to college.

2) People who like to get up early in the morning in order to drink more coffee is likely to become easily tired in the afternoon.

3) Hanging from the knob on the bedroom door, Tom thought the new shirt was his favorite.

4) I ran across the street to speak to her, then she surprised me by saying that she had bought a new car.

5) Its common for a magazine to have better sales if it mentions computers, handhelds or other new technology on it's cover.

6) Each student in the class who will take the series of exams on advanced mathematics need to study in advance.

7) Their are several reasons why there having problems with they're children.

8) You have to work hard to succeed at college, so each and every student need to devote time to their studies.

9) Completed on October 28, 1965 the Gateway Arch in St. Louis Missouri is dedicated to Thomas Jefferson who purchased the Louisiana Territory and made the Westward Expansion Movement possible.

10) Before leaving the building at night, please be sure to check the following – the lights, the locks and them storage lockers on the second floor.

11) Student's motivation levels are usually higher when they need to study for final exams.

12) Your phone call (which I told you not to make) interrupted me during an important meeting.

# Grammar and Punctuation – Answers

1) I haven't seen her or her sister since they went away to college.

2) People who like to get up early in the morning in order to drink more coffee are likely to become easily tired in the afternoon.

3) Hanging from the knob on the bedroom door, the new shirt was Tom's favorite.

4) I ran across the street to speak to her. Then she surprised me by saying that she had bought a new car.

5) It's common for a magazine to have better sales if it mentions computers, handhelds, or other new technology on its cover.

6) Each student in the class who will take the series of exams on advanced mathematics needs to study in advance.

7) There are several reasons why they're having problems with their children.

8) Students have to work hard to succeed at college, so each and every student needs to devote time to his or her studies.

9) Completed on October 28, 1965, the Gateway Arch in St. Louis, Missouri, is dedicated to Thomas Jefferson, who purchased the Louisiana Territory and made the Westward Expansion Movement possible.

10) Before leaving the building at night, please be sure to check the following: the lights, the locks, and those storage lockers on the second floor.

11) Students' motivation levels are usually higher when they need to study for final exams.

12) Your phone call, which I told you not to make, interrupted me during an important meeting.

# PART 5 – DEVELOPING YOUR SENTENCES

## How to Use Phrases, Clauses and Cohesive Devices to Develop Your Sentences

In order to perform well on the CBEST essay writing test, you will need to write essays that have advanced and developed sentence structures.

Sentence linking words, sometimes called cohesive devices, are words and phrases that are used in order to combine short sentences together to create more complex sentence structures.

Sentence linking words and phrases fall into three categories: sentence linkers, phrase linkers, and subordinators.

In order to understand how to use these types of sentence linking words and phrases correctly, you will need to know some basics of English grammar.

The basic grammatical principles for these concepts are explained in this section. Be sure to study the examples carefully before you attempt the exercises in the following section of the study guide.

TYPE 1 – SENTENCE LINKERS:

Sentence linkers are used to link two complete sentences together. A complete sentence is one that has a grammatical subject and a verb.

Sentence linkers are usually placed at the beginning of a sentence and are followed by a comma.

84

They can also be preceded by a semicolon and followed by a comma when joining two sentences together. When doing so, the first letter of the first word of the second sentence must not be capitalized.

Sentence linker examples:

You need to enjoy your time at college. *However*, you should still study hard.

You need to enjoy your time at college; *however*, you should still study hard.

In the examples above, the grammatical subject of the first sentence is "you" and the verb is "need to enjoy".

In the second sentence, "you" is the grammatical subject and "should study" is the verb.

TYPE 2 – PHRASE LINKERS:

In order to understand the difference between phrase linkers and sentence linkers, you must first be able to distinguish a sentence from a phrase.

A phrase linker must be followed by a phrase, while a sentence linker must be followed by a sentence.

The basic distinction between phrases and sentences is that phrases do not have both grammatical subjects and verbs, while sentences contain grammatical subjects and verbs.

*Here are some examples of phrases:*

Her beauty and grace

Life's little problems

A lovely summer day in the month of June

Working hard

Being desperate for money

Note that the last two phrases above use the –ing form, known in these instances as the present participle.

Present participle phrases, which are often used to modify nouns or pronouns, are sometimes placed at the beginning of sentences as introductory phrases.

*Here are some examples of sentences:*

Mary worked all day long.

My sister lives in Seattle.

Wintertime is brutal in Milwaukee.

"Mary," "my sister," and "wintertime" are the grammatical subjects of the above sentences.

Remember that verbs are words that show action or states of being, so "worked," "lives," and "is" are the verbs in the three sentences above.

Look at the examples that follow:

Phrase linker example 1 – no comma:

He received a promotion *because of* his dedication to the job.

"His dedication to the job" is a noun phrase.

Phrase linker example 2 – with comma:

*Because of* his dedication to the job, he received a promotion.

When the sentence begins with the phrase linker, we classify the sentence as an inverted sentence.

Notice that you will need to place a comma between the two parts of the sentence when it is inverted.

TYPE 3 – SUBORDINATORS:

Subordinators must be followed by an independent clause. Subordinators cannot be followed by a phrase.

The two clauses of a subordinated sentence must be separated by a comma.

The structure of independent clauses is similar to that of sentences because independent clauses contain a grammatical subject and a verb.

Subordinator examples:

*Although* he worked hard, he failed to make his business profitable.

He failed to make his business profitable, *although* he worked hard.

There are two clauses: "He worked hard" and "he failed to make his business profitable."

The grammatical subjects in each clause are the words "he", while the verbs are "worked" and "failed."

*Now look at the sentence linking words and phrases below. Note which ones are sentence linkers, which ones are phrase linkers, and which ones are subordinators.*

*Then refer to the rules above to remember the grammatical principles for sentence linkers, phrase linkers, and subordinators.*

Sentence linkers for giving additional information

further

furthermore

apart from this

what is more

in addition

additionally

in the same way

moreover

## Sentence linkers for giving examples

for example

for instance

in this case

in particular

more precisely

namely

in brief

in short

## Sentence linkers for stating the obvious

obviously

clearly

naturally

of course

surely

after all

## Sentence linkers for giving generalizations

in general

on the whole

as a rule

for the most part

generally speaking

in most cases

Sentence linkers for stating causes and effects

thus

accordingly

hence

therefore

in that case

under those circumstances

as a result

for this reason

as a consequence

consequently

in effect

Sentence linkers for concession or unexpected results

however

nevertheless

meanwhile

Sentence linkers for giving conclusions

finally

to conclude

lastly

in conclusion

Sentence linkers for contrast

on the other hand

on the contrary

alternatively

rather

Sentence linkers for paraphrasing or restating

in other words

that is to say

that is

Sentence linkers for showing similarity

similarly

in the same way

likewise

Phrase linkers for giving additional information

besides

in addition to

Phrase linkers for stating causes and effects

because of

due to

owing to

Phrase linkers for concession or unexpected results

despite

in spite of

Phrase linkers for comparison

compared to

like

Phrase linkers for contrast

in contrast to

instead of

rather than

without

Subordinators

although

as

because

but

due to the fact that

even though

since

so

once

unless

until

when

whereas

while

not only . . . but also

Time words that can be used both as phrase linkers and subordinators

after

before

<u>Special cases</u>

yet –"Yet" can be used as both a subordinator and as a sentence linker.

in order to – "In order to" must be followed by the base form of the verb.

thereby – "Thereby" must be followed by the present participle.

*We will look at the present participle and base forms in the following exercises.*

# Sentence Development Exercises

*Look at the pairs of sentences in the exercises below. Make new sentences, using the phrase linkers, sentence linkers, and subordinators provided. In many cases, you will need to create one single sentence from the two sentences provided. You may need to change or delete some of the words in the original sentences.*

## Exercise 1:

The temperature was quite high yesterday.

It really didn't feel that hot outside.

*Write new sentences beginning as follows:*

a) In spite of . . .

Hint: You need to change the form of the verb "was" in answer (a).

b) The temperature . . .

You need to include the word "nevertheless" in answer (b). Be careful with punctuation and capitalization in your answer.

## Exercise 2:

Our star athlete didn't receive a gold medal in the Olympics.

He had trained for competition for several years in advance.

*Write new sentences beginning as follows:*

a) Our star athlete . . . .

Answer (a) should contain the word "although."

b) Despite . . .

**Exercise 3:**

There are acrimonious relationships within our extended family.

Our immediate family decided to go away on vacation during the holiday season to avoid these conflicts.

*Write new sentences beginning as follows:*

a) Because of . . .

b) Because . . .

c) Due to the fact that . . .

**Exercise 4:**

My best friend had been feeling extremely sick for several days.

She refused to see the doctor.

*Write new sentences beginning as follows:*

a) My best friend . . .

Answer (a) should contain the word "however."

b) My best friend . . .

Answer (b) should contain the word "but."

Be careful with capitalization and punctuation in your answers.

**Exercise 5:**

He generally doesn't like drinking alcohol.

He will do so on social occasions.

*Write new sentences beginning as follows:*

a) While . . .

b) He generally . . .

Answer (b) should contain the word "yet."

**Exercise 6:**

The government's policies failed to stimulate spending and expand

economic growth.

The country slipped further into recession.

*Write new sentences beginning as follows:*

a) The government's policies . . .

Answer (a) should contain the word "thus."

b) The government's policies . . .

Answer (b) should contain the word "so."

**Exercise 7:**

Students may attend certain classes without fulfilling a prerequisite.

Students are advised of the benefit of taking at least one non-

required introductory course.

*Write new sentences beginning as follows:*

    a) Even though . . .

    b) Students may attend . . .

Answer (b) should contain the phrase "apart from this."

**Exercise 8:**

    There have been advances in technology and medical science.

    Infant mortality rates have declined substantially in recent years.

*Write new sentences beginning as follows:*

    a) Owing to . . .

    b) Since . . .

**Exercise 9:**

    It was the most expensive restaurant in town.

    It had rude staff and provided the worst service.

*Write new sentences beginning as follows:*

    a) It was the most . . .

Answer (a) should contain the word "besides."

    b) In addition to . . .

**Exercise 10:**

*Now try to combine these three sentences:*

The judge did not punish the criminal justly.

He decided to grant a lenient sentence.

He did not send out a message to deter potential offenders in the

future.

*Write new sentences as follows:*

a) Instead of . . . and thereby . . .

b) Rather than . . . in order to . . .

Before you attempt your answer, look for the cause and effect

relationships among the three sentences.

In other words, which event came first?

Which ones were second and third in the chain of events?

Also be careful with punctuation in your answers.

# Answers to the Sentence Development Exercises

**Exercise 1:**

**Answer (a)**

> In spite of the temperature being quite high yesterday, it really didn't feel that hot outside.

The words "in spite of" are a phrase linker, not a sentence linker.

That is to say, "in spite of" needs to be followed by a phrase, not a clause.

The verb "was" needs to be changed to "being" in order to form a present participle phrase.

Present participle phrases are made by using the –ing form of the verb.

We will see this construction again in some of the following answers.

**Answer (b)**

There are two possible answers.

> The temperature was quite high yesterday. Nevertheless, it really didn't feel that hot outside.

> The temperature was quite high yesterday; nevertheless, it really didn't feel that hot outside.

"Nevertheless" is a sentence linker. As such, it needs to be used to begin a new sentence.

Alternatively, the semicolon can be used to join the original sentences. If the semicolon is used, the first letter of the word following it must not be capitalized.

**Exercise 2:**

**Answer (a)**

Our star athlete didn't receive a gold medal in the Olympics, although he had trained for competition for several years in advance.

"Although" is a subordinator, so the two sentences can be combined without any changes.

**Answer (b)**

Despite having trained for competition for several years in advance, our star athlete didn't receive a gold medal in the Olympics.

"Despite" is a phrase linker. As we have seen in answer (a) of exercise 1 above, phrase linkers need to be followed by phrases, not clauses.

The two parts of the sentence are inverted, and the verb "had" needs to be changed to "having" to make the present participle form.

**Exercise 3:**

**Answer (a)**

> Because of acrimonious relationships within our extended family, our immediate family decided to go away on vacation during the holiday season to avoid these conflicts.

"Because of" is a phrase linker. As such, the subject and verb (there are) need to be removed from the original sentence in order to form a phrase.

**Answer (b)**

> Because there are acrimonious relationships within our extended family, our immediate family decided to go away on vacation during the holiday season to avoid these conflicts.

**Answer (c)**

> Due to the fact that there are acrimonious relationships within our extended family, our immediate family decided to go away on vacation during the holiday season to avoid these conflicts.

"Because" and "due to the fact that" are subordinators, so no changes to the original sentences are required.

The phrase "to avoid these conflicts" can be omitted since this idea is already implied by the words "acrimonious relationships."

**Exercise 4:**

**Answer (a)**

There are two possible answers.

> My best friend had been feeling extremely sick for several days. However, she refused to see the doctor.

> My best friend had been feeling extremely sick for several days; however, she refused to see the doctor.

Like "nevertheless" in exercise 1, the word "however" is a sentence linker. Remember that sentence linkers usually need to be used at the beginning of a new sentence.

Alternatively, the semicolon can be used to join the original sentences. If the semicolon is used, "however" must not begin with a capital letter and needs to be followed by a comma.

**Answer (b)**

> My best friend had been feeling extremely sick for several days, but she refused to see the doctor.

"But" is a subordinator, so the two sentences can be combined without any changes.

## Exercise 5:

### Answer (a)

> While he generally doesn't like drinking alcohol, he will do so on
> social occasions.

Like the word "although," the word "while" is a subordinator, so no
changes to the original sentences are needed.

### Answer (b)

"Yet" can be used as both a subordinator and as a sentence linker, so
there are three possible answers in this instance.

When used as a sentence linker, the sentence construction is similar to
the sentences containing nevertheless" from exercise 1 and "however"
from exercise 4.

Accordingly, the two following sentences are possible answers:

> He doesn't like drinking alcohol. Yet, he will do so on social
> occasions.

> He doesn't like drinking alcohol; yet, he will do so on social
> occasions.

A third possible answer is to use "yet" as a subordinator.

> He doesn't like drinking alcohol, yet he will do so on social
> occasions.

The difference is that the third sentence places slightly less emphasis on the particular occasions in which he will drink than the other two sentences.

**Exercise 6:**

**Answer (a)**

"Thus" is a sentence linker, so there are two possible answers.

> The government's policies failed to stimulate spending and expand economic growth. Thus, the country slipped further into recession.

> The government's policies failed to stimulate spending and expand economic growth; thus, the country slipped further into recession.

**Answer (b)**

> The government's policies failed to stimulate spending and expand economic growth, so the country slipped further into recession.

"So" is a subordinator. The two sentences may therefore be joined without any changes.

**Exercise 7:**

**Answer (a)**

There are two possible answers.

Even though students may attend certain classes without fulfilling a prerequisite, they are advised of the benefit of taking at least one non-required introductory course.

Even though students are advised of the benefit of taking at least one non-required introductory course, they may attend certain classes without fulfilling a prerequisite.

"Even though" is a subordinator, so no changes are needed. It is advisable to change the word "students" to the pronoun "they" on the second part of the new sentence in order to avoid repetition.

The order or the clauses may be changed in the new sentence since there is no cause and effect relationship between the two original sentences.

**Answer (b)**

There are two possible answers.

Students may attend certain classes without fulfilling a prerequisite. Apart from this, they are advised of the benefit of taking at least one non-required introductory course.

Students may attend certain classes without fulfilling a prerequisite; apart from this, they are advised of the benefit of taking at least one non-required introductory course.

"Apart from this" is a sentence linker, so it needs to be used at the beginning of a separate sentence.

**Exercise 8:**

**Answer (a)**

> Owing to advances in technology and medical science, infant mortality rates have declined substantially in recent years.

"Owing to" is a phrase linker that shows cause and effect. In this case the cause is advances in technology and medical science, and the effect or result is the decline in infant mortality rates.

Since "owing to" is a phrase linker, the grammatical subject of the original sentence (there) and the verb (have been) are removed when creating the new sentence.

**Answer (b)**

> Since there have been advances in technology and medical science, infant mortality rates have declined substantially in recent years.

"Since" is a subordinator, so you can combine the sentences without making any changes.

Remember to use the comma between the two parts of the sentence because the clauses have been inverted.

**Exercise 9:**

**Answer (a)**

It was the most expensive restaurant in town, besides having rude staff and providing the worst service.

"Besides" is a phrase linker, so use the present participle form of both verbs in the second original sentence. Accordingly, "had" becomes "having" and "provide" becomes "providing."

**Answer (b)**

There are two possible answers.

In addition to being the most expensive restaurant in town, it had rude staff and provided the worst service.

In addition to having rude staff and providing the worst service, it was the most expensive restaurant in town.

"In addition to" is a phrase linker, so the present participle forms are used in the phrase containing this word.

The order of the original sentences can be changed since there is no cause and effect relationship between these ideas.

**Exercise 10:**

**Answer (a)**

> Instead of punishing the criminal justly and thereby sending out a message to deter potential offenders in the future, the judge decided to grant a lenient sentence.

**Answer (b)**

> Rather than punishing the criminal justly in order to send out a message to deter potential offenders in the future, the judge decided to grant a lenient sentence.

As you can see, answers (a) and (b) above are somewhat similar in their construction.

"Instead of" and "rather than" need to be used with the present particle form (punishing).

"Thereby" must be followed by the present participle form (sending).

However, "in order to" needs to take the base form of the verb (send).

The base form is the verb before any change has been made to it, like making the –ed or –ing forms. The following are examples of base forms of verbs: eat, sleep, work, play.

## PART 6 – ESSAY CORRECTION EXERCISES

## ESSAY CORRECTION EXERCISE 1

*The draft essays that follow contain errors. Choose the correct version of each part of each sentence from the answer choices provided. If the part of the sentence is correct as written, you should choose answer A. The answers are provided at the end of the exercises.*

[1] Antarctica is a mysterious and remote continent [2] one which is often forgotten by virtue of its geographical location. [3] Now that the Antarctic is remote and desolate. [4] Nevertheless, an understanding of the organisms that inhabit this continent was critical [5] to our comprehension of the world as a global community. [6] For this reason, the southernmost continent has the source of a great deal of scientific investigation.

[7] Many notable recent research has come from America and Great Britain. [8] The British Antarctic Survey, sponsored with the Natural Environment Research Council of the United Kingdom, [9] and the United States Antarctic Resource Center, a collaborate of the United States Geological Survey Mapping Division and the National Science Foundation, [10] are forerunners in the burgeoning currently field of research in this area.

[11] This corpus of research has resulted in an abundance of factual data on the Antarctic. [12] For example, one now know that more than ninety nine percent of the land is completely covered by snow and ice, [13] which making Antarctica the coldest continent on the planet. [14] This inhospitable climate, has not surprisingly, brought about the adaptation [15] of a plethora of plants and biological organisms on the continent present. [16] An investigation for the sedimentary geological formations

provides testimony to the process of adaptation. [17] Ancient sediment's recovered from the bottom of Antarctic lakes, [18] bacteria as well as discovered in ice, [19] has reveal the history of climate change over the past 10,000 years.

Item 1.
A. Antarctica is a mysterious and remote continent
B. Antarctica is a mysterious and resounding continent
C. Antarctica is a mysterious and respectable continent
D. Antarctica is a mysterious and resistant continent
E. Antarctica is a mysterious and restrained continent

Item 2.
A. one which is often forgotten by virtue of its geographical location.
B. one whose often forgotten by virtue of its geographical location.
C. that is often forgotten by virtue of its geographical location.
D. this is often forgotten by virtue of its geographical location.
E. those are often forgotten by virtue of its geographical location.

Item 3.
A. Now that the Antarctic is remote and desolate.
B. Always, the Antarctic is remote and desolate.
C. Since the Antarctic is remote and desolate.

D. Indeed, the Antarctic is remote and desolate.
E. On the other hand, the Antarctic is remote and desolate.

Item 4.
A. Nevertheless, an understanding of the organisms that inhabit this continent was critical
B. Nevertheless, an understanding of the organisms that inhabit this continent were critical
C. Nevertheless, an understanding of the organisms that inhabit this continent is critical
D. Nevertheless, an understanding of the organisms that inhabit this continent are critical
E. Nevertheless, an understanding of the organisms that inhabit this continent are being critical

Item 5.
- A. to our comprehension of the world as a global community.
- B. to our comprehension at the world as a global community.
- C. to our comprehension in the world as a global community.
- D. to our comprehension about the world as a global community.
- E. to our comprehension for the world as a global community.

Item 6.
- A. For this reason, the southernmost continent has the source of a great deal of scientific investigation.
- B. For this reason, the southernmost continent has been the source of a great deal of scientific investigation.
- C. For this reason, the southernmost continent was the source of a great deal of scientific investigation.
- D. For this reason, the southernmost continent has to be the source of a great deal of scientific investigation.
- E. For this reason, the southernmost continent had the source of a great deal of scientific investigation.

Item 7.
- A. Many notable recent research has come from America and Great Britain.
- B. Much notable recent research has come from America and Great Britain.
- C. More notable recent research has come from America and Great Britain.
- D. More than notable recent research has come from America and Great Britain.
- E. As much as notable recent research has come from America and Great Britain.

Item 8.
- A. The British Antarctic Survey, sponsored with the Natural Environment Research Council of the United Kingdom,
- B. The British Antarctic Survey, sponsored by the Natural Environment Research Council of the United Kingdom,
- C. The British Antarctic Survey, sponsored against the Natural Environment Research Council of the United Kingdom,

D.   The British Antarctic Survey, sponsored from the Natural Environment Research Council of the United Kingdom,

E.   The British Antarctic Survey, sponsored upon the Natural Environment Research Council of the United Kingdom,

Item 9.

A.   and the United States Antarctic Resource Center, a collaborate of the United States Geological Survey Mapping Division and the National Science Foundation,

B.   And the United States Antarctic Resource Center, a collaborative of the United States Geological Survey Mapping Division and the National Science Foundation,

C.   and the United States Antarctic Resource Center, a collaboratively of the United States Geological Survey Mapping Division and the National Science Foundation,

D.   and the United States Antarctic Resource Center, a collaboration of the United States Geological Survey Mapping Division and the National Science Foundation,

E.   and the United States Antarctic Resource Center, a collaborator of the United States Geological Survey Mapping Division and the National Science Foundation,

Item 10.

A.   are forerunners in the burgeoning currently field of research in this area.

B.   are forerunners in the burgeoning field of currently research in this area.

C.   are currently forerunners in the burgeoning field of research in this area.

D.   are forerunners in the burgeoning field of research in currently this area.

E.   are forerunners in the burgeoning field of research in this currently area.

Item 11.

A.   This corpus of research has resulted in an abundance of factual data on the Antarctic.

B.   This corpus of research was resulted in an abundance of factual data on the Antarctic.

C.    This corpus of research has been resulted in an abundance of factual data on the Antarctic.

D.    This corpus of research was resulting in an abundance of factual data on the Antarctic.

E.    This corpus of research resulting in an abundance of factual data on the Antarctic.

Item 12.

A.    For example, one now know that more than ninety nine percent of the land is completely covered by snow and ice,

B.    For example, we now know that more than ninety nine percent of the land is completely covered by snow and ice,

C.    For example, they now knows that more than ninety nine percent of the land is completely covered by snow and ice,

D.    For example, the community now know that more than ninety nine percent of the land is completely covered by snow and ice,

E.    For example, the research now know that more than ninety nine percent of the land is completely covered by snow and ice,

Item 13.

A.    which making Antarctica the coldest continent on the planet.

B.    which is making Antarctica the coldest continent on the planet.

C.    making Antarctica the coldest continent on the planet.

D.    has made Antarctica the coldest continent on the planet.

E.    that made Antarctica the coldest continent on the planet.

Item 14.

A.    This inhospitable climate, has not surprisingly, brought about the adaptation

B.    This inhospitable climate has, not surprisingly, brought about the adaptation

C.    This inhospitable climate has, not surprisingly; brought about the adaptation

D.    This inhospitable climate has not surprisingly: brought about the adaptation

E.    This inhospitable climate has not surprisingly, brought about the adaptation

Item 15.
- A. of a plethora of plants and biological organisms on the continent present.
- B. of a plethora of plants and biological organisms present on the continent.
- C. of a plethora on the continent of plants and biological organisms present.
- D. of a plethora of plants on the continent and biological organisms present.
- E. of a plethora of plants and on the continent biological organisms present.

Item 16.
- A. An investigation for the sedimentary geological formations provides testimony to the process of adaptation.
- B. An investigation within the sedimentary geological formations provides testimony to the process of adaptation.
- C. An investigation at the sedimentary geological formations provides testimony to the process of adaptation.
- D. An investigation about the sedimentary geological formations provides testimony to the process of adaptation.
- E. An investigation into the sedimentary geological formations provides testimony to the process of adaptation.

Item 17.
- A. Ancient sediment's recovered from the bottom of Antarctic lakes,
- B. Ancient sediments' recovered from the bottom of Antarctic lakes,
- C. Ancient sediments recovered from the bottom of Antarctic lakes,
- D. Ancient's sediment recovered from the bottom of Antarctic lakes,
- E. Ancient's sediments recovered from the bottom of Antarctic lakes,

Item 18.
- A. bacteria as well as discovered in ice,
- B. as well as bacteria discovered in ice,
- C. bacteria discovered as well as in ice,

D.     bacteria discovered in as well as ice,

E.     bacteria discovered in ice as well,

Item 19.

A.     has reveal the history of climate change over the past 10,000 years.

B.     has revealed the history of climate change over the past 10,000 years.

C.     have reveal the history of climate change over the past 10,000 years.

D.     have revealed the history of climate change over the past 10,000 years.

E.     have been revealed the history of climate change over the past 10,000 years.

Item 20.

If the student were to add a paragraph at the end of the essay explaining that the reliability of the research on Antarctica has been disputed, the essay would lose:

A.     its academic tone.

B.     its clarity and focus.

C.     the sense that this topic of current interest.

D.     its emphasis on the inhospitality of the Antarctic climate.

E.     the sense of importance it places on the scientific evidence.

## ESSAY CORRECTION EXERCISE 2

[1] The major significant characteristic of any population is its age-sex structure, [2] defining as the proportion of people of each gender in each different age group. [3] The age-sex structure determines the potential for reproduction, [4] and for example population growth, [5] based on the balance of males and females of child-bearing age inside a population. [6] Thus, the age-sex structure was social policy implications.

[7] For instance, a population with a high proportion of citizens elderly [8] needs to consider its governmental-funded pension schemes and health care systems carefully. [9] As follows: a demographic with a greater

percentage of young children should ensure [10] which its educational funding and child welfare policies are implemented efficaciously.

[11] Accordingly, as the composition of a population changes against time, [12] the government may need to restate its funding priorities.

[13] For it is possible that a population may have low birth rates [14] resulting an imbalance in the age-sex structure. [15] Low birth rate's might also be attributable to governmental policy that attempts to control the population. [16] Policies are one example of that restrict the number of children a family can have this outcome.

[17] Other possible reason for these types of demographic changes might be unnaturally high death rates, [18] such like in the case of a disease epidemic or natural disaster. [19] Finally, migration is another factor [20] in demographic attrition, because in any population, a certain amount of people, may decide to emigrate, or move to a different country.

Item 1.
- A. The major significant characteristic of any population is its age-sex structure,
- B. The majorly significant characteristic of any population is its age-sex structure,
- C. The most significantly characteristic of any population is its age-sex structure,
- D. The most significant characteristic of any population is its age-sex structure,
- E. The more significant characteristic of any population is its age-sex structure,

Item 2.
- A. defining as the proportion of people of each gender in each different age group.
- B. defined as the proportion of people of each gender in each different age group.

C.  which defining as the proportion of people of each gender in each different age group.
D.  which defined as the proportion of people of each gender in each different age group.
E.  as defined as the proportion of people of each gender in each different age group.

Item 3.
A.  The age-sex structure determines the potential for reproduction,
B.  The age-sex structure determined the potential for reproduction,
C.  The age-sex structure has determined the potential for reproduction,
D.  The age-sex structure had determined the potential for reproduction,
E.  The age-sex structure was determined the potential for reproduction,

Item 4.
A.  and for example population growth,
B.  and so that population growth,
C.  and with regard to population growth,
D.  and it follows that population growth,
E.  and as a consequence population growth,

Item 5.
A.  based on the balance of males and females of child-bearing age inside a population.
B.  based on the balance of males and females of child-bearing age within a population.
C.  based on the balance of males and females of child-bearing age containing  a population.
D.  based on the balance of males and females of child-bearing age consisting a population.
E.  based on the balance of males and females of child-bearing age attributing a population.

Item 6.
A.  Thus, the age-sex structure was social policy implications.
B.  Thus, the age-sex structure is social policy implications.
C.  Thus, the age-sex structure has social policy implications.

D.     Thus, the age-sex structure had social policy implications.

E.     Thus, the age-sex structure does social policy implications.

Item 7.

A.     For instance, a population with a high proportion of citizens elderly

B.     For instance, a population with an elderly high proportion of citizens

C.     For instance, a population with a high proportion elderly of citizens

D.     For instance, a population with a high proportion of elderly citizens

E.     For instance, a population with a high elderly proportion of citizens

Item 8.

A.     needs to consider its governmental-funded pension schemes and health care systems carefully.

B.     needs to consider its governmentally-funded pension schemes and health care systems carefully.

C.     needs to consider its funded-governmental pension schemes and health care systems carefully.

D.     needs to consider its funded-governmentally pension schemes and health care systems carefully.

E.     needs to consider its funded governmentally-pension schemes and health care systems carefully.

Item 9.

A.     As follows: a demographic with a greater percentage of young children should ensure

B.     Just as a demographic with a greater percentage of young children should ensure

C.     Conversely, a demographic with a greater percentage of young children should ensure

D.     Despite, a demographic with a greater percentage of young children should ensure

E.     Unless a demographic with a greater percentage of young children should ensure

Item 10.
- A. which its educational funding and child welfare policies are implemented efficaciously.
- B. that its educational funding and child welfare policies are implemented efficaciously.
- C. which it's educational funding and child welfare policies are implemented efficaciously.
- D. that it's educational funding and child welfare policies are implemented efficaciously.
- E. hence its educational funding and child welfare policies are implemented efficaciously.

Item 11.
- A. Accordingly, as the composition of a population changes against time,
- B. Accordingly, as the composition of a population changes for time,
- C. Accordingly, as the composition of a population changes over time,
- D. Accordingly, as the composition of a population changes past time,
- E. Accordingly, as the composition of a population changes as time,

Item 12.
- A. the government may need to restate its funding priorities.
- B. the government may need to re-evaluate its funding priorities.
- C. the government may need to recuperate its funding priorities.
- D. the government may need to cooperate its funding priorities.
- E. the government may need to instigate its funding priorities.

Item 13.
- A. For it is possible that a population may have low birth rates
- B. For this possible that a population may have low birth rates
- C. This is possible that a population may have low birth rates
- D. It is possible that a population may have low birth rates
- E. That is possible that a population may have low birth rates

Item 14.
  A.    resulting an imbalance in the age-sex structure.
  B.    because an imbalance in the age-sex structure.
  C.    due to an imbalance in the age-sex structure.
  D.    since an imbalance in the age-sex structure.
  E.    in order to imbalance in the age-sex structure.

Item 15.
  A.    Low birth rate's might also be attributable to governmental
        policy that attempts to control the population.
  B.    Low birth's rates might also be attributable to governmental
        policy that attempts to control the population.
  C.    Low births' rates might also be attributable to governmental
        policy that attempts to control the population.
  D.    Low birth rates' might also be attributable to governmental
        policy that attempts to control the population.
  E.    Low birth rates might also be attributable to governmental policy
        that attempts to control the population.

Item 16.
  A.    Policies are one example of that restrict the number of children
        a family can have this outcome.
  B.    Policies that restrict are one example of the number of children
        a family can have this outcome.
  C.    Policies that restrict the number of children a family can have
        this outcome are one example.
  D.    Policies that restrict the number of children a family can have
        are one example of this outcome.
  E.    Policies that restrict the number of children a family are one
        example of this outcome can have.

Item 17.
  A.    Other possible reason for these types of demographic changes
        might be unnaturally high death rates,
  B.    Others possible reason for these types of demographic changes
        might be unnaturally high death rates,
  C.    Another possible reason for these types of demographic
        changes might be unnaturally high death rates,
  D.    Anothers possible reason for these types of demographic
        changes might be unnaturally high death rates,
  E.    Another possible reasons for these types of demographic
        changes might be unnaturally high death rates,

Item 18.
    A.    such like in the case of a disease epidemic or natural disaster.
    B.    such as in the case of a disease epidemic or natural disaster.
    C.    as such as in the case of a disease epidemic or natural disaster.
    D.    as its in the case of a disease epidemic or natural disaster.
    E.    as much like as in the case of a disease epidemic or natural disaster.

Item 19.
    A.    Finally, migration is another factor
    B.    Final migration is another factor
    C.    Final, migration is another factor
    D.    To end, migration is another factor
    E.    Conclusively, migration is another factor

Item 20.
    A.    in demographic attrition, because in any population, a certain amount of people, may decide to emigrate, or move to a different country.
    B.    in demographic attrition because in any population a certain amount of people may decide to emigrate, or move to a different country.
    C.    in demographic attrition because, in any population, a certain amount of people may decide to emigrate or move to a different country.
    D.    in demographic attrition because in any population, a certain amount of people may decide to emigrate, or move to a different country.
    E.    in demographic attrition because in any population a certain amount of people may decide to emigrate or move to a different country.

Item 21.
Suppose that the student was asked to write an essay, the purpose of which was to explain how the government could rectify current deficiencies in the age-sex structure. Has the student achieved this purpose?
    A.    Yes, because the student talks about the government's reassessment of funding priorities.

B.     Yes, because the student describes the social policy implication of the age-sex structure.

C.     Yes, because the student explains the effect of governmental policy on low birth rates.

D.     No, because the student fails to provide sufficient examples of the how governmental policy needs to adapt to population changes over time.

E.     No, because the student does not enumerate specific solutions that the government could attempt.

## ESSAY CORRECTION EXERCISE 3

[1] A group of English separatists known as the Pilgrims first left England to live in Amsterdam, in 1608. [2] After spending a few years in their new city, apart from this, many members of the group [3] felt whose they did not have enough independence. [4] Hence, in 1617, the Pilgrims decided to leave Amsterdam immigrating to America.

[5] More of these separatists were poor farmers [6] whom did not have much education or social status, and, not surprisingly, [7] the group had many financial problems that prevented them for beginning their journey. [8] Thereby their inability to finance themselves caused many disputes and disagreements, [9] the Pilgrims finally managing to obtain financing [10] from a well-known and considerable London businessman named Thomas Weston.

[11] Having secured Weston's monetary support, the group returned to England to pick up some additional passengers, [12] and it boarded a large ship called the Mayflower on September 16, 1620. [13] After 65 days at sea, the pilgrim's reached America.

[14] Plymouth a town about 35 miles southeast of Boston in the New England state of Massachusetts [15] was established by the Pilgrims in

December 21, 1620. [16] Even though the early days of this new lives were filled with hope and promise, [17] the harsh winter proved being too much for some of the settlers. [18] Near half of the Pilgrims died during that first winter, [19] but those who lived go on to work hard and prosper.

Item 1.
A. A group of English separatists known as the Pilgrims first left England to live in Amsterdam, in 1608.
B. A group of English separatists known as the Pilgrims first left England to live, in Amsterdam, in 1608.
C. A group of English separatists known as the Pilgrims first left England to live in Amsterdam in 1608.
D. A group of English separatists known as the Pilgrims, first left England to live in Amsterdam, in 1608.
E. A group of English separatists known as the Pilgrims, first left England to live, in Amsterdam in 1608.

Item 2.
A. After spending a few years in their new city, apart from this, many members of the group
B. After spending a few years in their new city, in this case, many members of the group
C. After spending a few years in their new city, namely, many members of the group
D. After spending a few years in their new city, however, many members of the group
E. After spending a few years in their new city, otherwise, many members of the group

Item 3.
A. felt whose they did not have enough independence.
B. felt whom they did not have enough independence.
C. felt which they did not have enough independence.
D. felt that they did not have enough independence.
E. felt in that they did not have enough independence.

Item 4.
 A. Hence, in 1617, the Pilgrims decided to leave Amsterdam immigrating to America.
 B. Hence, in 1617, the Pilgrims decided to leave Amsterdam to immigrate to America.
 C. Hence, in 1617, the Pilgrims decided to leave Amsterdam emigrating to America.
 D. Hence, in 1617, the Pilgrims decided to leave Amsterdam to emigrate to America.
 E. Hence, in 1617, the Pilgrims decided to leave Amsterdam for migrating to America.

Item 5.
 A. More of these separatists were poor farmers
 B. Much of these separatists were poor farmers
 C. Many of these separatists were poor farmers
 D. Many more of these separatists were poor farmers
 E. The most of these separatists were poor farmers

Item 6.
 A. whom did not have much education or social status, and, not surprisingly,
 B. of whom did not have much education or social status, and, not surprisingly,
 C. whose did not have much education or social status, and, not surprisingly,
 D. which did not have much education or social status, and, not surprisingly,
 E. who did not have much education or social status, and, not surprisingly,

Item 7.
 A. the group had many financial problems that prevented them for beginning their journey.
 B. the group had many financial problems that prevented them to beginning their journey.
 C. the group had many financial problems that prevented them from beginning their journey.
 D. the group had many financial problems that prevented them against beginning their journey.

125

E.      the group had many financial problems that prevented them with beginning their journey.

Item 8.
  A.    Thereby their inability to finance themselves caused many disputes and disagreements,
  B.    Although their inability to finance themselves caused many disputes and disagreements,
  C.    Nevertheless their inability to finance themselves caused many disputes and disagreements,
  D.    Despite their inability to finance themselves caused many disputes and disagreements,
  E.    In spite of their inability to finance themselves caused many disputes and disagreements,

Item 9.
  A.    the Pilgrims finally managing to obtain financing
  B.    the Pilgrims finally managed obtaining financing
  C.    the Pilgrims finally were managed obtaining financing
  D.    the Pilgrims finally were managed to obtain financing
  E.    the Pilgrims finally managed to obtain financing

Item 10.
  A.    from a well-known and considerable London businessman named Thomas Weston.
  B.    From a well-known and affluent London businessman named Thomas Weston.
  C.    from a well-known and unfortunate London businessman named Thomas Weston.
  D.    from a well-known and adamant London businessman named Thomas Weston.
  E.    from a well-known and insistent London businessman named Thomas Weston.

Item 11.
  A.    Having secured Weston's monetary support, the group returned to England to pick up some additional passengers,
  B.    To have secured Weston's monetary support, the group returned to England to pick up some additional passengers,

C.     They have secured Weston's monetary support, the group returned to England to pick up some additional passengers,

D.     When they have secured Weston's monetary support, the group returned to England to pick up some additional passengers,

E.     Having secured Weston's monetary support, the group returned to England to pick up some additional passengers

Item 12.

A.     and it boarded a large ship called the Mayflower on September 16, 1620.

B.     and he or she boarded a large ship called the Mayflower on September 16, 1620.

C.     and one boarded a large ship called the Mayflower on September 16, 1620.

D.     and they boarded a large ship called the Mayflower on September 16, 1620.

E.     and those boarded a large ship called the Mayflower on September 16, 1620.

Item 13.

A.     After 65 days at sea, the pilgrim's reached America.

B.     After 65 days at sea, the Pilgrims' reached America.

C.     After 65 days at sea, the Pilgrims reached America.

D.     After 65 days at sea, Pilgrim's reached America.

E.     After 65 days at sea, Pilgrims' reached America.

Item 14.

A.     Plymouth a town about 35 miles southeast of Boston in the New England state of Massachusetts

B.     Plymouth, a town about 35 miles southeast of Boston in the New England state of Massachusetts,

C.     Plymouth, a town about 35 miles southeast of Boston in the New England, state of Massachusetts

D.     Plymouth, a town about 35 miles southeast of Boston in the New England, state of Massachusetts,

E.     Plymouth, a town about 35 miles southeast of Boston, in the New England, state of Massachusetts,

Item 15.

A.     was established by the Pilgrims in December 21, 1620.

B.    was established by the Pilgrims on December 21, 1620.
C.    was established by the Pilgrims at December 21, 1620.
D.    was established by the Pilgrims upon December 21, 1620.
E.    was established by the Pilgrims during December 21, 1620.

Item 16.
A.    Even though the early days of this new lives were filled with hope and promise,
B.    Even though the early days of that new lives were filled with hope and promise,
C.    Even though the early days of their new lives were filled with hope and promise,
D.    Even though the early days of these new live were filled with hope and promise,
E.    Even though the early days of those new live were filled with hope and promise,

Item 17.
A.    the harsh winter proved being too much for some of the settlers.
B.    the harsh winter proved to be too much for some of the settlers.
C.    the harsh winter proved to being too much for some of the settlers.
D.    the harsh winter proved been too much for some of the settlers.
E.    the harsh winter proved to been too much for some of the settlers.

Item 18.
A.    Near half of the Pilgrims died during that first winter,
B.    Nearly half of the Pilgrims died during that first winter,
C.    Nearly of half of the Pilgrims died during that first winter,
D.    Near of half of the Pilgrims died during that first winter,
E.    Almost near half of the Pilgrims died during that first winter,

Item 19.
A.    but those who lived go on to work hard and prosper.
B.    but those who lived goes on to work hard and prosper.
C.    but those who lived going on to work hard and prosper.
D.    but those who lived went on to work hard and prosper.
E.    but those who lived had went on to work hard and prosper.

Item 20.

If the student removed the last sentence of the essay, how would this affect the essay?

    A.    The essay would have more emphasis on the hardships of the Pilgrims.

    B.    The comments on the early days of the Pilgrims would have increased importance.

    C.    The historical account of the Pilgrims would lack continuity.

    D.    The essay would lack a sense of focus.

    E.    The essay would lack a proper conclusion.

## ESSAY CORRECTION EXERCISE 4

[1] In 1929 that electrical activity in the human brain was first discovered.

[2] Hans Berger, the German psychiatrist made the discovery, [3] was despondent to find out, in contrast to, that his research was quickly dismissed by many other scientists.

[4] The work of Berger was confirmed three years later, in 1932, when Edgar Adrian a Briton, [5] clearly demonstrated that the brain, like the heart, is profuse in its electrical activity. [6] Because of Adrian's work, it know that the electrical impulses [7] in the brain called brain waves are a mixture of four different frequencies, [8] that are based on the number of electrical impulses [9] that occurring in the brain per second.

[10] Accordingly, there are four types of brain waves as follows, alpha, beta, delta, and theta.  [11] Alpha waves occur in a state of relaxation, while beta waves occur when a person is alert. [12] In addition, delta waves take place for sleep, but they can also occur dysfunctionally when the brain has been severely damaged. [13] Finally, theta waves are a frequency of [14] somewhere in between alpha and delta. [15] Seems that the purpose of theta waves is solely to facilitate the combination of the other brain waves.

[16] The whole notion of brain waves feeds into the current controversy about brain death. [17] Some believe that brain death is characterized by the failure of the cerebral cortex to function. [18] On the other hand, anothers say that mere damage to the cerebral cortex is not enough. [19] They assert that brain stem function must also cease before can a person be declared dead because the cerebral cortex is responsible for other bodily processes.

Item 1.
  A.   In 1929 that electrical activity in the human brain was first discovered.
  B.   It in 1929 that electrical activity in the human brain was first discovered.
  C.   It was in 1929 that electrical activity in the human brain was first discovered.
  D.   It in 1929 was that electrical activity in the human brain was first discovered.
  E.   That in 1929 electrical activity in the human brain was first discovered.

Item 2.
  A.   Hans Berger, the German psychiatrist made the discovery,
  B.   Hans Berger, the German psychiatrist had made the discovery,
  C.   Hans Berger, the German psychiatrist who made the discovery,
  D.   Hans Berger, the German psychiatrist whom made the discovery,
  E.   Hans Berger, the German psychiatrist which made the discovery,

Item 3.
  A.   was despondent to find out, in contrast to, that his research was quickly dismissed by many other scientists.
  B.   was despondent to find out, likewise, that his research was quickly dismissed by many other scientists.
  C.   was despondent to find out, but, that his research was quickly dismissed by many other scientists.

D. was despondent to find out, though, that his research was quickly dismissed by many other scientists.

E. was despondent to find out, although, that his research was quickly dismissed by many other scientists.

Item 4.

A. The work of Berger was confirmed three years later, in 1932, when Edgar Adrian a Briton,

B. The work of Berger was confirmed three years later, in 1932, when Edgar Adrian, a Briton,

C. The work of Berger was confirmed three years later, in 1932, when Edgar Adrian a Briton

D. The work of Berger was confirmed three years later, in 1932, when Edgar Adrian a Briton;

E. The work of Berger was confirmed three years later, in 1932, when Edgar Adrian, a Briton;

Item 5.

A. clearly demonstrated that the brain, like the heart, is profuse in its electrical activity.

B. demonstrated that the clearly brain, like the heart, is profuse in its electrical activity.

C. demonstrated that the brain, like clearly the heart, is profuse in its electrical activity.

D. demonstrated that the brain, like the heart clearly, is profuse in its electrical activity.

E. demonstrated that the brain, like the heart, is profuse clearly in its electrical activity.

Item 6.

A. Because of Adrian's work, it know that the electrical impulses

B. Because of Adrian's work, it known that the electrical impulses

C. Because of Adrian's work, it is known that the electrical impulses

D. Because of Adrian's work, we known that the electrical impulses

E. Because of Adrian's work, one known that the electrical impulses

Item 7.
- A. in the brain called brain waves are a mixture of four different frequencies,
- B. in the brain, called brain waves are a mixture of four different frequencies,
- C. in the brain called brain waves, are a mixture of four different frequencies,
- D. in the brain, called brain waves, are a mixture of four different frequencies,
- E. in the brain, called brain waves, are a mixture, of four different frequencies,

Item 8.
- A. that are based on the number of electrical impulses
- B. that based on the number of electrical impulses
- C. which are based on the number of electrical impulses
- D. which based on the number of electrical impulses
- E. are based on the number of electrical impulses

Item 9.
- A. that occurring in the brain per second.
- B. that occurred in the brain per second.
- C. that had occurred in the brain per second.
- D. that have occurrence in the brain per second.
- E. that occur in the brain per second.

Item 10.
- A. Accordingly, there are four types of brain waves as follows, alpha, beta, delta, and theta.
- B. Accordingly, there are four types of brain waves as follows: alpha, beta, delta, and theta.
- C. Accordingly, there are four types of brain waves as follows; alpha, beta, delta, and theta.
- D. Accordingly, there are four types of brain waves as follows alpha, beta, delta, and theta.
- E. Accordingly, there are four types of brain waves as follows. Alpha, beta, delta, and theta.

Item 11.
- A. Alpha waves occur in a state of relaxation, while beta waves occur when a person is alert.
- B. Alpha waves occur in a state of relaxation, rather beta waves occur when a person is alert.
- C. Alpha waves occur in a state of relaxation, rather than beta waves occur when a person is alert.
- D. Alpha waves occur in a state of relaxation, instead of waves occur when a person is alert.
- E. Alpha waves occur in a state of relaxation, as for beta waves occur when a person is alert.

Item 12.
- A. In addition, delta waves take place for sleep, but they can also occur dysfunctionally when the brain has been severely damaged.
- B. In addition, delta waves take place during sleep, but they can also occur dysfunctionally when the brain has been severely damaged.
- C. In addition, delta waves take place since sleep, but they can also occur dysfunctionally when the brain has been severely damaged.
- D. In addition, delta waves take place with sleep, but they can also occur dysfunctionally when the brain has been severely damaged.
- E. In addition, delta waves take place at sleep, but they can also occur dysfunctionally when the brain has been severely damaged.

Item 13.
- A. Finally, theta waves are a frequency of
- B. Finally, theta waves are of a frequency
- C. Finally, theta waves of are a frequency
- D. Finally, of theta waves are a frequency
- E. Finally, theta waves are a of frequency

Item 14.
- A. somewhere in between alpha and delta.
- B. somewhere with between alpha and delta.
- C. somewhere in besides alpha and delta.

133

D.     somewhere at between alpha and delta.
E.     somewhere at besides alpha and delta.

Item 15.
A.     Seems that the purpose of theta waves is solely to facilitate the combination of the other brain waves.
B.     Seemingly that the purpose of theta waves is solely to facilitate the combination of the other brain waves.
C.     It seemingly that the purpose of theta waves is solely to facilitate the combination of the other brain waves.
D.     It is seemingly that the purpose of theta waves is solely to facilitate the combination of the other brain waves.
E.     It seems that the purpose of theta waves is solely to facilitate the combination of the other brain waves.

Item 16.
A.     The whole notion of brain waves feeds into the current controversy about brain death.
B.     The whole notion of brain waves feeds at the current controversy about brain death.
C.     The whole notion of brain waves feeds with the current controversy about brain death.
D.     The whole notion of brain waves feeds against the current controversy about brain death.
E.     The whole notion of brain waves feeds for the current controversy about brain death.

Item 17.
A.     Some believe that brain death is characterized by the failure of the cerebral cortex to function.
B.     Some people's belief that brain death is characterized by the failure of the cerebral cortex to function.
C.     Some peoples' belief that brain death is characterized by the failure of the cerebral cortex to function.
D.     Certain peoples believe that brain death is characterized by the failure of the cerebral cortex to function.
E.     Certain believe that brain death is characterized by the failure of the cerebral cortex to function.

Item 18.
- A. On the other hand, anothers say that mere damage to the cerebral cortex is not enough.
- B. On the other hand, another say that mere damage to the cerebral cortex is not enough.
- C. On the other hand, others say that mere damage to the cerebral cortex is not enough.
- D. On the other hand, other say that mere damage to the cerebral cortex is not enough.
- E. On the other hand, other's say that mere damage to the cerebral cortex is not enough.

Item 19.
- A. They assert that brain stem function must also cease before can a person be declared dead because the cerebral cortex is responsible for other bodily processes.
- B. They assert that brain stem function must also cease before a person can be declared dead because the cerebral cortex is responsible for other bodily processes.
- C. They assert that brain stem function must also cease before may a person be declared dead because the cerebral cortex is responsible for other bodily processes.
- D. They assert that brain stem function must also cease before might a person can be declared dead because the cerebral cortex is responsible for other bodily processes.
- E. They assert that brain stem function must also cease before a person declared dead because the cerebral cortex is responsible for other bodily processes.

Item 20.
Imagine that the student would like to add the following sentence to the essay. What is the best location for this sentence?
Therefore, for these myriad reasons, it has become very important to measure brain activity.
- A. At the end of the first paragraph.
- B. At the end of the second paragraph.
- C. At the end of the third paragraph.
- D. At the beginning of the last paragraph.
- E. At the end of the last paragraph.

## ESSAY CORRECTION EXERCISE 5

[1] Cancer, a group of mainly than 100 different types of disease,
[2] occurs where cells in the body begin to divide abnormally and continue dividing and forming more cells without control or order. [3] All internal organs of the body consist of cells, which normally divide to produce more cells when the body requires them. [4] This is a natural, orderly process, that keeps human beings healthy.

[5] If a cell divides when is not necessary, a large growth called a tumor can form. [6] These tumors can usually be removed, and in many cases, they do not recurrence. [7] Unfortunately, in some cases the cancer at the original tumor spreads. [8] The spread of cancer in such way is called metastasis.

[9] There are some factors which are being known to increase the risk of cancer. [10] Smoking is the single cause largest of death from cancer in the United States. [11] One-third of the death's from cancer each year are related to smoking, [12] making tobacco use the most preventable cause of death in this country.

[13] Choice of food can also be link to cancer. [14] Research shows that there are a link between high-fat food and certain cancers, and being seriously overweight is also a cancer risk. [15] Cancer risk can be reduced with a cut down on fatty food and eating generous amounts of fruit and vegetables.

Item 1.
  A.    Cancer, a group of mainly than 100 different types of disease,
  B.    Cancer, a group of more than 100 different types of disease,
  C.    Cancer, a group of 100 more different types of disease,
  D.    Cancer, a group of mostly than 100 different types of disease,

E.     Cancer, a group of almost than 100 different types of disease,

Item 2.
  A.     occurs where cells in the body begin to divide abnormally and
         continue dividing and forming more cells without control or
         order.
  B.     occurs which cells in the body begin to divide abnormally and
         continue dividing and forming more cells without control or
         order.
  C.     occurs in which cells in the body begin to divide abnormally and
         continue dividing and forming more cells without control or
         order.
  D.     occurs when cells in the body begin to divide abnormally and
         continue dividing and forming more cells without control or
         order.
  E.     occurs once when cells in the body begin to divide abnormally
         and continue dividing and forming more cells without control or
         order.

Item 3.
  A.     All internal organs of the body consist of cells, which normally
         divide to produce more cells when the body requires them.
  B.     All internal organs of the body consist of cells, which divide to
         normally produce more cells when the body requires them.
  C.     All internal organs of the body consist of cells, which divide to
         produce more normally cells when the body requires them.
  D.     All internal organs of the body consist of cells, which divide to
         produce more cells when normally the body requires them.
  E.     All internal organs of the body consist of cells, which divide to
         produce more cells when the body requires them normally.

Item 4.
  A.     This is a natural, orderly process, that keeps human beings
         healthy.
  B.     This is a natural, orderly process that keeps human beings
         healthy.
  C.     This is a natural orderly process, that keeps human beings
         healthy.
  D.     This is a natural orderly process that keeps human beings
         healthy.

E.    This is a natural orderly, process that keeps human beings
      healthy.

Item 5.
   A.    If a cell divides when is not necessary, a large growth called a
         tumor can form.
   B.    If a cell divides when they are not necessary, a large growth
         called a tumor can form.
   C.    If a cell divides when it is not necessary, a large growth called a
         tumor can form.
   D.    If a cell divides when are not necessary, a large growth called a
         tumor can form.
   E.    If a cell divides when that not necessary, a large growth called a
         tumor can form.

Item 6.
   A.    These tumors can usually be removed, and in many cases, they
         do not recurrence.
   B.    These tumors can usually be removed, and in many cases, they
         do not make recurrence.
   C.    These tumors can usually be removed, and in many cases, they
         do not recurring.
   D.    These tumors can usually be removed, and in many cases, they
         do not are recurred.
   E.    These tumors can usually be removed, and in many cases, they
         do not recur.

Item 7.
   A.    Unfortunately, in some cases the cancer at the original tumor
         spreads.
   B.    Unfortunately, in some cases the cancer from the original tumor
         spreads.
   C.    Unfortunately, in some cases the cancer with the original tumor
         spreads.
   D.    Unfortunately, in some cases the cancer for the original tumor
         spreads.
   E.    Unfortunately, in some cases the cancer below the original
         tumor spreads.

Item 8.
- A.   The spread of cancer in such way is called metastasis.
- B.   The spread of cancer in such a way is called metastasis.
- C.   The spread of cancer in such ways is called metastasis.
- D.   The spread of cancer in such like way is called metastasis.
- E.   The spread of cancer in such like ways is called metastasis.

Item 9.
- A.   There are some factors which are being known to increase the risk of cancer.
- B.   There are some factors which are know to increase the risk of cancer.
- C.   There are some factors which are knowing to increase the risk of cancer.
- D.   There are some factors which are known to increase the risk of cancer.
- E.   There are some factors which have known to increase the risk of cancer.

Item.10
- A.   Smoking is the single cause largest of death from cancer in the United States.
- B.   Smoking is the single cause of largest death from cancer in the United States.
- C.   Smoking is the single cause of death largest from cancer in the United States.
- D.   Smoking is the single cause of death from cancer largest in the United States.
- E.   Smoking is the largest single cause of death from cancer in the United States.

Item 11.
- A.   One-third of the death's from cancer each year are related to smoking,
- B.   One-third of the deaths' from cancer each year are related to smoking,
- C.   One-third of the deaths from cancer each year are related to smoking,
- D.   One-third of cancer's deaths each year are related to smoking,
- E.   One-third of cancers' deaths each year are related to smoking,

Item 12.
- A. making tobacco use the most preventable cause of death in this country.
- B. which making tobacco use the most preventable cause of death in this country.
- C. made tobacco use the most preventable cause of death in this country.
- D. which will be making tobacco use the most preventable cause of death in this country.
- E. in making tobacco use the most preventable cause of death in this country.

Item 13.
- A. Choice of food can also be link to cancer.
- B. Choice of food can also be linking to cancer.
- C. Choice of food can also be linked to cancer.
- D. Choice of food can also been linked to cancer.
- E. Choice of food can also link to cancer.

Item 14.
- A. Research shows that there are a link between high-fat food and certain cancers, and being seriously overweight is also a cancer risk.
- B. Research shows that there is a link between high-fat food and certain cancers, and being seriously overweight is also a cancer risk.
- C. Research shows that there's links between high-fat food and certain cancers, and being seriously overweight is also a cancer risk.
- D. Research shows that there is existing a link between high-fat food and certain cancers, and being seriously overweight is also a cancer risk.
- E. Research shows that there in existence a link between high-fat food and certain cancers, and being seriously overweight is also a cancer risk.

Item 15.
- A. Cancer risk can be reduced with a cut down on fatty food and eating generous amounts of fruit and vegetables.
- B. Cancer risk can be reduced with cutting down on fatty food and eating generous amounts of fruit and vegetables.
- C. Cancer risk can be reduced with cutting down fatty food and eating generous amounts of fruit and vegetables.
- D. Cancer risk can be reduced by cutting down on fatty food and eating generous amounts of fruit and vegetables.
- E. Cancer risk can be reduced by cut down on fatty food and eating generous amounts of fruit and vegetables.

Item 16.
Suppose the student wants to include an admonition to the reader about how he or she can prevent cancer risks. Which sentence, if added to the end of the essay, would achieve this purpose?
- A. Accordingly, the government needs to act now to help improve the health of the country.
- B. Militating against the causes of cancer is a difficult but necessary task.
- C. It is therefore the responsibility of each individual to try to mitigate cancer risk by living a healthy lifestyle.
- D. However, these deaths could easily have been avoided.
- E. Nevertheless, most people agree that trying to prevent cancer risk is extremely important.

**ASWERS TO THE ESSAY CORRECTION EXERCISES**

**Antarctica Essay**

1. A

2. C

3. D

4. C

5. A

6. B

7. B

8. B

9. D

10. C

11. A

12. B

13. C

14. B

15. B

16. E

17. C

18. B

19. D

20. E

**Population Age-Sex Structure Essay**

1. D

2. B

3. A

4. E

5. B

6. C

7. D

8. B

9. C

10. B

11. C

12. B

13. D

14. C

15. E

16. D

17. C

18. B

19. A

20. D

21. E

## The Pilgrims Essay

1.  C
2.  D
3.  D
4.  D
5.  C
6.  E
7.  C
8.  B
9.  E
10. B
11. A
12. D
13. C
14. B
15. B
16. C
17. B
18. B
19. D
20. E

**Brain Wave Research Essay**

1. C

2. C

3. D

4. B

5. A

6. C

7. D

8. C

9. E

10. B

11. A

12. B

13. B

14. A

15. E

16. A

17. A

18. C

19. B

20. E

**Cancer Risk Essay**

1. B

2. D

3. A

4. B

5. C

6. E

7. B

8. B

9. D

10. E

11. C

12. A

13. C

14. B

15. D

16. C

Made in the USA
Las Vegas, NV
01 December 2023

81932993R00085